D1025119

Praise for *Surviving Your Serengeti*

"A rare book in management literature. Enjoyable, informative read, with clear applications to be successful."

—John Ullmen, PhD,
UCLA Anderson School of Management

"The perfect 'visual' experience to simulate the skills required to take your mastery of business to the next level. I could not put this book down!"

—Mark Willis,
CEO, Keller Williams Realty International

"A terrific book filled with adventure and wisdom that will touch your life and increase your personal effectiveness. I enjoyed it immensely."

—Bob Burg,
National Best-Selling Author of
The Go-Giver* and *Go-Givers Sell More

"*Surviving Your Serengeti* is an exciting journey about life and business for any age, young and old."

—Dale Stinton,
CEO, National Association of Realtors®

"It takes more than good business sense to survive changing economies and this impactful book will inspire readers to pursue their dreams and overcome seemingly impossible odds."

—Dave Liniger,
Founder and Chairman, RE/MAX International

"Superb! Swanepoel shows he can write business fables as well as he does real estate trends. Exciting and educational, all wrapped into one experience."

—Alex Perriello,
President and CEO,
Realogy Franchise Group

"An instant classic! Discover the very best strategies to navigate through difficult times!"

—Tom Ferry,
CEO, YourCoach.com and Author of the
New York Times* Best-Seller *Life! By Design

"This compelling story is masterfully written. I recommend this book unreservedly for anyone wanting to fine-tune their success plan!"

—Don Hutson,
CEO, U.S. Learning, and Coauthor of the
New York Times* Best-Seller, *The One Minute
Entrepreneur* and *The One Minute Negotiator

"AWESOME! An excellent story. I've found myself thinking about *Surviving Your Serengeti* in the middle of doing other things."

—Michael McClure,
President and CEO, Professional One

"Incredible perspective on life's challenges and how to maneuver through them successfully."

—Gary Danielson,
CBS Commentator and Former NFL
Quarterback

Surviving
YOUR
SERENGETI

Surviving
YOUR
SERENGETI

7 Skills to Master Business and Life

A FABLE OF SELF-DISCOVERY

STEFAN SWANEPOEL

WILEY

John Wiley & Sons, Inc.

Published by John Wiley & Sons, Inc., Hoboken, New Jersey.
Published simultaneously in Canada.

For general information on our other products and services or for technical support, please contact our Customer Care Department within the United States at (800) 762-2974, outside the United States at (317) 572-3993 or fax (317) 572-4002.

Wiley also publishes its books in a variety of electronic formats. Some content that appears in print may not be available in electronic books. For more information about Wiley products, visit our web site at www.wiley.com.

Library of Congress Cataloging-in-Publication Data:

Swanepoel, Stefan.
    Surviving your serengeti : 7 skills to master business and life / Stefan Swanepoel.
       p. cm.
    ISBN 978-0-470-94780-7 (cloth)
    ISBN 978-1-118-00857-7 (ebk)
    ISBN 978-1-118-00858-4 (ebk)
    ISBN 978-1-118-00859-1 (ebk)
    1. Success. 2. Life skills. 3. Survival skills. 4. Industrial efficiency. I. Title.
    BJ1611.2.S85   2011
    650.1—dc22

                                                                          2010039905

Printed in the United States of America
10 9 8 7 6 5 4 3 2

To everyone who lives with focus, enthusiasm, and purpose.
Specifically to my Zachariah, my mentor and Dad.

CONTENTS

INTRODUCTION

During my formative years in Africa, I developed deep feelings for the surrounding nature and wildlife; they became a part of me, and I of them. But as I became an adult and turned my attention to the world of business, I left Africa and the Serengeti behind to immigrate to America.

It was not until a recent visit to the Serengeti Plains of East Africa that I reconnected with this unique refuge. Simply put, it is the last sanctuary for the greatest concentration of wildlife remaining on earth.

Nearly two million wildebeest, zebras, and gazelles annually run a 1,000-mile journey filled with hunger, thirst, predators, and exhaustion. The journey is so incomparably dangerous and massive that it is often rated the number one natural wonder of the world.

For me, this journey is a parable for success. It's a window into the very meaning of life that provides a simple way to understand, appreciate, and remember the basic skills that all living beings need to survive and thrive.

For most of us, the world we live in today is, of course, a far cry from the Serengeti. Television, the Internet, mobile media, fast food, and many more innovations comprise a society dominated by a demand for speed, comfort, and instant gratification. We continue to advance technology, only to find ourselves spinning through one "solution" after the other. We face global financial and economic challenges that stretch our resources and shape our professional and personal lives as never before.

The obstacles that those who live and die on the Serengeti face are, in many ways, no different than the challenges we face at the office or at home every day. While our trials certainly take place in a different realm, the seven skills that the animals use to overcome their harsh conditions can also help us rise above our own adversities.

It is my hope that this fable will reaffirm that:

- Everyone can survive his or her own personal Serengeti, no matter the challenges.
- No journey is ever too long.
- Nothing is impossible.

—STEFAN SWANEPOEL

Chapter 1

ARRIVAL IN AFRICA

"Where am I?" Sean Spencer thought as he peered out of the dirty Plexiglas window at the vast open expanse below.

The droning of the airplane's engine lulled him deeper into his thoughts. Though he knew how much this trip meant to his wife Ashley, he couldn't just forget about everything. The recent loss of her teaching job and his struggle to keep his company afloat placed their whole livelihood on the line. This trip—which she'd won as a rookie salesperson of the year—couldn't have come at a worse time.

The pilot nudged the throttle as the wheels of the small six-seat Cessna grazed the top of a large acacia tree and came to rest on a narrow dirt strip. As the propeller carved its last arc against the late afternoon sun and yellow dust settled around them, Sean wondered again where exactly they'd landed. Surely this wasn't an airport. The landing strip was hard to distinguish from the surrounding veldt. It didn't even have a building—just one old weather-beaten wind sock.

He sat back and took in the scenery around them as the heat rose inside the plane. There wasn't much to see except a single Land Rover parked a short distance away at the edge of the clearing. He smiled to himself as he looked at Ashley sitting in the seat next to the pilot.

Like a little kid on a new adventure, she absorbed every detail with wonder on her face—and she wasn't going to waste a minute of it.

As he climbed out of the side door and rubbed his stiff back, he instinctively took out his BlackBerry and squinted at the screen in the glaring afternoon sun. He sighed and shrugged his shoulders—no bars. This was going to be a long three days without communication. His company's recent proposal for a large solar generating system in California's central valley was under review, and he was concerned they would be underbid again. Without this business, he was worried that he'd have to make further cutbacks.

"Sean!" Ashley shouted. She was already standing next to the driver of the Land Rover, waving him over.

As he approached the vehicle, a young man dressed in green khaki shorts extended his hand. "Greetings Mr. Spencer; welcome to the Serengeti. I'm Raymond. I'll be your guide for the next couple of days. Help yourself to a cold drink from the icebox while I take care of your luggage," he yelled over his shoulder, already on his way to the plane.

Ashley noted the distant look on Sean's face. "Isn't this awesome? We're in Africa! Can you believe it? Have you ever seen anything so majestic? What do you say we just clear our minds of all our problems and enjoy the trip?"

This was something Sean had always admired and even envied in his wife: her ability to seamlessly adapt and enjoy what she was doing without any interruption. To her, Los Angeles and all their troubles simply didn't exist right now. She could shut out whatever she chose, and focus on where she was in that instance.

Ashley put her arm on Sean's shoulder. "I promise you all our problems will still be there when we get back," she said.

Sean smiled. "I'm sure they will." Like it or not, his dead BlackBerry would force him to give it a shot—for her sake, if nothing else.

"The pilot says he'll be back in three days," Raymond exclaimed, after he stashed their bags in the back of the Land Rover and opened the front door. Sean gave Ashley the front seat and clamored into the back with the gear.

He tried to focus on the passing panorama as Raymond headed for camp, but his mind kept reminding him of all that had been left unfinished at the office. Success hadn't come easily for Sean, and the company he'd enjoyed building had become the very thing that consumed him. The first-class team he had gathered needed guidance and inspiration now more than ever before. In fact, the *last* thing his employees needed right now was for him to be thousands of miles away, completely out of touch.

"How long have you been a guide?" Ashley asked Raymond.

"It's been seven years since I completed my training." Raymond smiled with pride.

"How long does the training take?"

"To become a certified guide, you have to undergo a minimum of four years of study and practical hands-on experience before you are ready to get your own Land Rover. I grew up right here on the Serengeti, so it's always been a central part of me all my life."

"We're lucky to have you," Ashley said, admiring Raymond's dedication.

Raymond began to tell them about his home as he navigated the Rover. "The Serengeti," sweeping his arm in a wide arc, "is predominantly a plateau of endless plains and grassy savannahs. It is one huge ecosystem that spans over 10,000 square miles, spreading over two countries,

Tanzania and Kenya. Right now, we're camped in the south-central part of the park in an area called Senoera. Over there in the east are the mountains, including the one everyone knows—Mount Kilimanjaro. She is an inactive volcano and Africa's highest peak at 19,330 feet above sea level. Because the location of Mount Kilimanjaro is so close to the equator, one encounters almost every climate on earth as you ascend from the valley floor to the peak, which remains covered with snow all year round."

Ashley couldn't take her eyes off the vast expanse of Africa being unveiled around every turn. "This is absolutely stunning. I've never seen anything like it."

Raymond smiled and continued. "In the west are various lakes, with Lake Victoria—the largest tropical lake in the world—being the most famous, and the source of the longest branch of the Nile River."

Raymond looked at Sean in the rearview mirror and beamed as if he was talking about his most prized possession. "The region has been blessed with an abundance of natural diversity that cannot be found anywhere else on the planet. For that reason, it has received World Heritage status as a biosphere ecology reserve."

As they rolled deeper into the bush, Sean and Ashley began to take in the wild breath of Africa. A subtly intoxicating sense of freedom and exhilaration came over them.

"I didn't expect it to be so hot this late in the day. Does it ever cool down?" Sean asked, draining a bottle of water.

"Yes, just as soon as the sun goes down," Raymond replied. "You'll feel the difference tonight at supper."

"Is this what the weather's like all the time?" asked Sean as he wiped his forehead for the umpteenth time.

"No," Raymond said as he continued to share more interesting snippets of information. They found themselves being drawn into the moment, despite the constant plume of dust rising up from the tires that slipped in one window and out the other, coating everything and everyone.

As they climbed a low rise, the sun was just barely hanging above the horizon. It painted the entire skyline with an inconceivable palette of reds, oranges, and yellows. Raymond pulled the Rover under a large acacia tree pointing his finger straight west into the setting sun. In the distance, silhouetted by the horizon, grazed a huge herd of animals. Ashley and Sean could hear the grunting, snorting, and occasionally the sound of hooves against the hard, sunbaked ground. Everywhere they looked, as far as they could see, the plains were filled with animals.

Sean was absolutely amazed. "I've seen the Serengeti savannahs on the Discovery Channel—but the real thing. Wow, it's so much bigger than I ever envisioned."

They got out of the Rover to stretch their legs and Raymond handed them a pair of binoculars. "Those are white-bearded wildebeest. You'll also see some zebras and gazelles." For the next 10 minutes no one said a word; they simply stood in awe of the abundance of animals—the ocean of life mingling together, prancing and tossing their heads as they moved in rhythm.

Raymond rested his arms on the open car door and broke the silence. "The wildebeest are the dominant species; they far outnumber any other animal on the Serengeti. Since the wildebeest prefer areas that are neither too wet nor too dry, they are constantly in search of a balance between the two. Their strong dependence on water and constant migration makes them a constant target for many predators.

"So, as if by nature's silent command, more than one-and-a-half million zebras, wildebeest, and gazelles leave the savannahs here on the southern plains and move through the woodlands to the western corridor, where the wildflowers are coming into bloom. Then from Lake Victoria they will curve back northward toward the sweet grass of the Masai Mara in Kenya. As the rains return life back here on the Serengeti savannahs, the great herds will migrate south and come back here where they started."

Ashley stared at the vast herds and handed the binoculars to Sean. "I never dreamed of seeing so many animals in one place—let alone within a few hours of arriving in Africa!"

Suddenly, a small group of about 100 wildebeest came running from behind them, swerving around the trees and anthills, leaping across the road heading toward the larger herd. They all ran in a single line, carefully preserving as much of the grass as possible. Sean and Ashley stood motionless as they watched the animals gallop a mere 10 yards in front of the Land Rover. There were no bars or fences; they were truly free in their natural habitat.

"Look at their muscular, front-heavy appearance with that distinctively large muzzle," Raymond continued. "See how their prominent horns are shaped like parentheses, extending outward to the side and then curving back inward, sort of like putting a bracket around that elongated snout of theirs. Based on their odd outward appearance you would never cast them as the animal species that would dominate the largest wildlife refuge on the planet."

"No, you definitely wouldn't," Ashley said. "It's a far cry from our society, where appearance means so much."

"Never judge a book by its cover, especially one as dusty as this one," Raymond said as he opened the door for Ashley.

"Incredible is the only word that can describe it," Ashley remarked. "Absolutely incredible."

Raymond smiled as he started the engine once again. "We need to move along if we're going to make it to the camp before dark."

The sound of grunts and snorts began to die down as they drove away from the herd. The last colors of sunset were draining from the western sky—it was only then that Sean and Ashley noticed that the oppressive heat was giving way to the chill of the night air. The dark was arriving quickly and soon Raymond was navigating some unseen path without headlights. Sean peered ahead, trying to discern some form of a road or trail, but it was as dark as the inside of an inkwell. "Why are you driving without lights?"

"Headlights would blind the wildebeest running across the road—and the last thing we need is to have one run into us. Driving in the dark lets the animals see us more easily and as we are the strangers here, it is best we stay out of their way and not intrude on their territory."

Raymond dodged another acacia branch that seemed to jump out of nowhere before making one final turn into a clearing. Suddenly, Sean and Ashley could see the outline of several tents ahead, silhouetted against the night by the warm glow of a campfire. Home at last— wherever that was. For now, home was a place that didn't belong to man—where wild animals ruled, and civilization had no purpose and little value.

> *"In the distance grazed tens of thousands of animals. Never in their wildest dreams could they have imagined the vastness of the Serengeti stretching out for miles and miles before them."*

Sean checked his BlackBerry again—still no bars. He was concerned about his colleagues back at the office even though he had seen them all this past week. But since there really wasn't much he could do about it, Sean switched his phone off and gazed out into the veldt.

This African jungle was so completely unlike the concrete jungle, he thought. Unspoiled, unscarred, and controlled by an entirely different set of rules. Everyone was forced to abide by nature's laws, with all of their wonderful yet harsh realities.

As Raymond pulled up in front of a large tent, they saw a number of people sitting around a campfire. A huge man approached from the dark and introduced himself.

"Welcome to the Serengeti, Mr. and Mrs. Spencer. My name is Aly. It is my pleasure to see to your every need while you are with us here at the Senoera camp. We have prepared your tent, and your luggage will be dropped there within a few minutes. Let me escort you to your new home so that you may freshen up before supper."

As they walked behind him, Aly pointed out a family of baboons perched in a tree. As Sean and Ashley approached the tent, the sight brought them up short. This wasn't a small tent. This was a spacious, well-equipped tent with two rooms and an enclosed toilet and shower section.

"Remember to put on something warm before you return for supper." With that, Aly bowed slightly and disappeared.

"Well," Sean said as he closed the tent flap behind them and looked at the bowls of steaming hot water along with a set of freshly wrapped soap and towels that would make even a five-star hotel blush. "This is the second time I've been impressed today."

Free of the afternoon's dust and ready for supper, Sean and Ashley stepped out of their tent. Nearby a choir of crickets and frogs pierced the darkness and they heard laughter in the distance. The evening chill swirled around them as they walked toward the glow of the campfire. They were glad to be wearing the sweaters that had been neatly laid out for them on the bed, since neither of them had thought to pack warm clothes for a trip to the tropics.

The freshly fed fire was crackling; its warm glow lit the small circle of camp chairs around it. The scent of something aromatic and spicy drifted from the cooking tent.

As they approached, Aly came walking toward them. "Mr. and Mrs. Spencer. I trust you found everything in your tent to your liking?"

"Absolutely," replied Ashley. "Everything is just perfect."

"Wonderful. May I get you a sundowner before supper?"

"Sundowner?" Sean frowned.

"Ah yes, it's how we end the day here in Africa, a drink before supper to smooth out the wrinkles of the day—we have Budweiser, Castle Lager, or perhaps a glass of wine?"

"Let's try the wine," Ashley suggested to Sean.

"Most certainly; may I suggest a Pinotage, a deep red wine from Southern Africa?"

"Thank you."

"While we get your drinks, let me introduce you to our other guests."

Aly led them closer to the fire where two other couples were engaged in a lively discussion. As they walked into the light of the fire the others rose from their camp chairs and Aly made the introductions.

"May I present your fellow campers, Mr. and Mrs. Johnson from Montana, and Mr. and Mrs. Cruz from New York."

With that, a huge man in his late sixties thrust his hand out to Sean. "Hi, I'm Dave Johnson and this is my wife, Mary."

Sean smiled in return. "I'm Sean and this is Ashley. We're from LA."

"We were just discussing who beat the Patriots in '05—was it the Panthers or the Eagles?"

"Give it a rest, Dave," said a young man in his mid-thirties, stepping forward and shaking Sean's hand.

"Hi, Sean, I'm Anthony Cruz, and this is Cecilia. Welcome to our little group. We've been wondering who the empty chairs were for."

"Are you with the mystery man?" asked Dave.

"Mystery man?" Sean repeated.

"Dave, let the man sit down before you drag him into your continual barrage of questions."

Without blinking, Sean responded, "By the way, the Patriots won over the Eagles—the only other team besides the Cowboys to win three Super Bowls in four years."

"Yeah, yeah. See? I told you, Anthony," Dave bolstered.

Sean had a knack for numbers and easily remembered different facts and figures—something that had always served him well in business. They were great conversation starters and provided him the ability to effortlessly communicate with anyone.

As they were warming up by the fire, Cecilia asked, "So Ashley, how did you two wind up coming to the Serengeti?"

"Well, actually, I won it. I started about a year ago as a sales consultant at a large multilevel marketing firm, and was fortunate to win rookie salesperson of the year. We had our choice of destinations: Hawaii or Africa. Even though Sean would rather be on the beach, I felt this was a once-in-a-lifetime opportunity—even if it was only for three days."

"Congratulations, that's awesome," Cecilia and Mary both chimed in.

Mary was easily twice Cecilia's age, but both women had warm and engaging smiles.

Dave got up and went over to the table to freshen his drink.

"So, Sean, have you met the mystery man yet?" he asked.

"No—who is this mysterious man you keep talking about? We just arrived this afternoon and have only met Raymond and Aly."

"Well, there's another man in camp. He's really tall. We've seen him twice, but only from a distance. He's neither a guest nor member of the crew. He leaves really early in the morning and returns long after sunset when the camp is closed down for the night. It all seems very secretive."

"What type of business are you in, Sean?" Anthony asked, changing the subject.

"Renewable energy. Started my own company a while back. We're involved in the planning and development of solar power systems for small and mid-sized companies. It's a fascinating field, but business has been slow recently. How about you guys?"

"Talk about slow," responded Anthony sarcastically. "Until recently, I thought I had a bright future in banking. But as a result of the economy, I'm among the millions of unemployed."

"Sorry to hear that, Anthony. I can really relate to how difficult it must be," Sean said.

"Thanks. And after applying for more than 40 jobs and still finding nothing, I needed a break. Cecilia suggested we come to Africa to participate on a mission trip arranged by our church, which starts next week."

"That's wonderful. And you, Dave?" Sean prompted.

"Well, after a lifetime in the Navy, I couldn't find a way to wrangle myself into the cockpit any longer—and the thought of a desk job didn't sit very well with me. So retirement offered me a chance to do something different."

"What's that?"

"About five years ago, Mary and I bought a franchise with one of the large real-estate companies. Unfortunately, the market took a beating. As you know, housing has been pretty lousy the last couple of years."

"Times are definitely tough," Sean said, as he thought about his own company's poor cash flow and low morale. Everyone had his or her own unique set of challenges in life.

Chapter 2

THE ENDURING WILDEBEEST

Aly came over to the fire with a five-minute supper call.

"Hey Aly, is our man of intrigue joining us tonight?" asked Dave.

"I don't know, Mr. Johnson. He isn't back yet."

"Back from where?"

"You'll have to ask him that."

"See? Even Aly is secretive about it."

As they were finishing up their drinks, a Jeep drove into the compound. Everyone turned when they heard the footsteps of someone heading down the path. The man who approached was slender and tall—well over six feet five—and appeared to have distinctively gray hair, though it was hard to tell at night. As he came closer to the light of the fire, Sean noticed something vaguely familiar about him.

Aly started to make the introductions. "This is my . . ."

Suddenly, Sean called out, "Zachariah! Zachariah Makena!"

The mystery man turned toward Sean with a smile that seemed to brighten his whole face. "Yes?"

"It's me, Sean Spencer."

The others looked at Sean in complete surprise as he warmly shook the mystery man's hand.

"Sean Spencer! What in the world are you doing out here in the heart of Africa? The last time I saw you was in England."

"That was 30 years ago," Sean said.

"Indeed. What have you being doing since finishing your studies?"

"Well, after graduating I received an offer from Anderson Consulting, did some work in Singapore, and then settled in the United States developing solar thermal power plants. Later, I started my own renewable energy company in California. What about you?"

"My plan was always to return to Africa. First, I did some conservation work . . ."

Realizing that everyone was staring at them, Sean quickly turned to make the introductions. "Sorry, Zachariah,

I would like you to meet my wife Ashley, and the other guests we just met tonight—Anthony and Cecilia Cruz, and Dave and Mary Johnson. Guys, let me introduce an old acquaintance of mine, Zachariah Makena. We attended the London School of Economics together in the early 1980s. Zachariah graduated a year ahead of me, but we shared a room during my first term. Back then he offered to show me Africa one day. I never thought I'd actually end up here."

At that moment, Aly stepped out of the shadows and led them to supper.

Upon arriving at dinner, another surprise awaited Sean and Ashley. Stretched out inside the mess tent was a long table covered with a linen tablecloth, set with china, and topped off with freshly cut flowers. Tall men dressed in white robes with bright red sashes and red felt fezes stood at each side of the table.

Once they were all seated, Aly signaled toward the side of the room. Seemingly, from out of nowhere, a salad buffet, soup, and meat entrée arrived on the table. The kitchen staff had outdone themselves, right down to the last detail.

After a while, Sean topped off their glasses and asked Zachariah, "So tell me what happened after London."

"I had several great offers to work in the United States, but I realized after thinking it through that I just couldn't picture myself away from Africa. There is a part of me that would never be happy away from the bush. It's too much a part of who I am.

"So I returned home to Nairobi and worked for the African Wildlife Foundation to protect the land in the Masai Steppe Heartland, where I gained a deep appreciation for the vital role each animal has in the circle of life. Increasingly, I began to realize that much of what we had learned in business school seemed to correlate to various aspects of nature. So, after a couple years, some friends and I formed a company to study unique animal skills."

Sean smiled as he thought back over his own life. He suddenly remembered that they had both made a vow to begin their own companies. Once he had started there had been no turning back. He was so focused and driven. But as the years passed, the more entangled he had become in administrative bureaucracy. Now, he felt trapped in the very company he had created. But could he change course? For some unexplained reason, the company and the team weren't firing on all cylinders— but he needed to push forward and find a solution. Now he was in Africa, of all places, sitting next to an old acquaintance. Seeing Zachariah again had given the trip an unexpected turn.

"Now it's your turn to answer—what brought you out here to the Serengeti?" Zachariah asked.

"Well, after the financial markets collapsed, it seemed as though no one was safe anymore. Thousands of companies laid off millions of people when the U.S. economy tanked."

"Yes, I know; we felt the ripple effects of your recession even here," Zachariah nodded.

"Well, unfortunately, Ashley was one of the casualties. About a year ago, she lost her job at the school that Crystal and Cathy, our two daughters, attended. Luckily, she didn't stay unemployed long. She quickly jumped into a multilevel marketing company, and became one of their best. Her salesperson of the year prize was this very trip."

"Excellent."

"Well, mind you, we also had a choice of Hawaii, which I would have preferred, but she picked the Serengeti. And now that you're here, I'm delighted she did."

"Thank you—what a great choice! You've certainly come at a fantastic time. With the dry season here, the wildebeest migration is just beginning. You no doubt must have seen many herds coming in today."

"We did—thousands. Which reminds me—what 'animal skills' were you referring to when we were discussing your company's objectives and areas of study?"

Although he usually didn't mingle with Aly's guests, this time was different; he knew Sean. He was looking forward to sharing some of the knowledge he had uncovered since university, and to get Sean's reaction.

"Let's adjourn to the campfire before I share some information about the wildebeest that I think you'll find very interesting," Zachariah said, as he stood up from the table.

Raymond placed more wood on the fire and new flames leapt into the dark sky. Zachariah looked at the enquiring faces now illuminated by the firelight.

"Alright, Zachariah, we are all ears," Sean said.

"Well, imagine it's a beautiful February morning under an infinite royal blue sky here in the Serengeti. The scenery still includes a hint of colorful orange clouds left over from the dawn, much like we had today. The temperature grows cooler as autumn sets in, much to the wildebeest's relief. Yet cooling temperatures also mean that winter is approaching, and with it, the dry season. Since wildebeest need water daily, this forces them to migrate."

It's interesting that even though the wildebeest outnumber all the other animals in this, the largest concentration of wildlife remaining on earth, they are still very vulnerable. The 1,000-mile journey they are forced to undertake every year offers no guarantees and hundreds of thousands of wildebeest will die. There is no certainty that there will be rain over the next hill, or for that matter that they will even make it over that hill. It's simply just a matter of moving forward."

"It's a great story, Zachariah," Ashley interrupted.

"It's more than a story, Ashley. It's about understanding their world as a means to gaining insight into our own. Consider the immense odds that the wildebeest have to overcome on their journey, as well as the endurance and resilience required to overcome each day's challenges—and you will begin to identify the wildebeest's distinctive skill."

Zachariah stared into the flickering flames before continuing.

"Think about the migration in different terms for a moment; imagine it to be a road map for your life. It illustrates the challenges, threats, changing environment, and shifting paradigms that we all encounter. The Serengeti shows us how different animals each possess a unique survival skill—skills that we all need to master in our own lives, but usually don't."

The group huddled closer to the glowing embers like little kids around a campfire listening to ghost stories. Zachariah picked up the coffee urn and walked around refilling everyone's cups as he continued.

"As we began studying each animal's particular skills, we developed techniques to better comprehend our own strengths and weaknesses. We learned how to apply them and gain the most from each skill."

"I'm confused," someone broke in. "Are you saying that people are like animals?"

"No, of course not," Zachariah replied, smiling. "But we all possess skills that we don't know we have, or never fully develop. What makes the Serengeti exceptional is that it isolates the core survival skills so unmistakably."

Mary looked up from her coffee. "So how do I find out what my core survival skill is?"

"Before you can determine that, you first need to encounter each animal in its natural surroundings and then fully comprehend what enables it to survive. Let's take a closer look at the central character of the migration— the wildebeest. You saw hundreds of them today, and

> *"Endurance is the steadfast capacity to hold on for one more day."*

while there are probably a number of abilities you could identify, there is one skill that truly sets them apart from the rest."

"What's that?" Sean asked.

"Think. Visualize their journey. Remember that every year, millions of them individually and collectively confront fear head-on and face thirst, hunger, exhaustion, and predation. Their core skill has enabled them not only to survive, but thrive. They have succeeded to such an extent that today they are the animal with the largest numbers in the Serengeti, thereby allowing them to dominate the entire region."

"Are you saying, then, that in spite of all that danger, the wildebeest have become the dominant species of the Serengeti because of their endurance?" Sean asked.

"Exactly. When the going gets tough, many of us give up; it's often far too easy to shift the blame, make excuses, or give ourselves reasons for failing to complete the task at hand. The absence of tenacity diminishes our ability to overcome our personal Serengeti."

"So, you're saying that we should learn to be more unrelenting?" Anthony asked.

"Yes. People frequently give up too soon. Everyone has his or her own personal Serengeti to survive: job loss, divorce, or an illness, for example. However, people who exhibit single-minded determination understand that it's often not the fastest or the strongest one that wins the race—it's the one that stays the course and goes the full distance," Zachariah continued.

Keep in mind, though, that you always need to pace yourself. Pushing yourself beyond your capacity to rebound from setbacks will cause you to wind up like a sprinter trying to run a marathon—exhausted and left in the dust. On the other hand, understanding your limits and working within them will allow you to stay the course till the end."

Zachariah looked at the group. "Who here can recall an instance where endurance has impacted their life?"

Dave, who had been sitting quietly, stood up. "I do. I remember a time in the Navy. There were a lot of strong petty officers that had the ability to keep focused and press on during the war. Though the tasks they were given seemed unattainable at times, they kept at it— and their resolute attitude would rub off on the young sailors. They would pick up on this outlook as they worked alongside the seasoned veterans. I can now see the wildebeest in many of them; they had a strong commitment to keep going, no matter what, and to endure some of life's most difficult challenges."

I also saw it in the American workforce during the financial meltdown. Despite the fact that we faced an entirely different set of circumstances, there was a similar sense of tenacity present. Folks all across the country had to worry about whether they'd be able to pay the mortgage, have a job next month, or even have food on the table. They faced fear and uncertainty. Many put in countless additional work hours or took a significant pay cut. It's really inspiring to see someone stay the course all the way."

"Beautiful," Zachariah responded. "Endurance is exactly that—your fighting spirit. It's what makes us get back up when we get knocked down.

"It also helps us deal with the tremendous stress of today's work environment. Everyone is pressured to get more done faster and at a lower cost. And it doesn't stop there. We receive these kinds of demands at home as well, with a resulting tension that affects everyone involved—employees, team members, families, and especially spouses. In simple terms, we really only have two options here: create barriers to hide behind, or find the strength to resolve the issues we face. While staying the course in and of itself is obviously not a guarantee for success, it is the number one skill that will see you through to the end."

"But what if we can't find it within ourselves?" Anthony asked.

"Then you need a spouse, close friend, or office colleague who can give you encouragement and motivation on a regular basis. Enduring together is much easier. Remember, the wildebeest doesn't run alone."

Aly glanced at his watch and decided it was time to interrupt the discussion. "Zach, it's getting late, and our guests need to be up early tomorrow morning. Raymond has a big day planned for you all tomorrow at the Simba Kopjes, the Hippo Pools, and the Rock Paintings. And if any of you haven't already seen the big five—lion, leopard, elephant, rhino, and buffalo—I'm sure you will see many of them tomorrow."

"Aly's right," Zachariah exclaimed, as he stood up and placed his empty coffee cup on the table. "I need to leave for the Grumeti River at four in the morning. There is a large herd of wildebeest that has been building up there since yesterday, and we anticipate a large river crossing tomorrow. Since it'll be the first major crossing of the year, I need to get an accurate count to compare with last year's stats. This will help us determine how the lead herd size has changed."

"Will you be back tomorrow evening?" Sean inquired.

"Yes," Zachariah responded, "but the time will depend on whether the wildebeest herd crosses the river by noon. Perhaps we can pick up our conversation again tomorrow if I am back. I've enjoyed meeting all of you, and Sean— what a treat to make contact again after so many years. But, I'm afraid you'll have to excuse me now," Zachariah said, bowing slightly and heading off into the night.

"What an intriguing man," Dave said, the expression on his face mirroring the wheels spinning in his mind. "Identifying your unique skill from the animals—that's an extraordinary concept."

"It's really fascinating," Cecilia responded. "The wildebeest basically have to face their own recession every year."

Turning to Sean, she exclaimed, "And you know our mystery man!"

"I do. Well, I *did*. I didn't know Zachariah was the mystery man. And this isn't the Zachariah I knew in London. He's changed a lot."

"So have you." Ashley smiled as she put her arm in Sean's. "It's been 30 years, you know."

"Yes, I suppose you're right. But there is really something very different about him that's more than just age—something I can't quite identify. Even back then, he was very astute. But it's not just his knowledge or intellect. It's almost as if he was speaking *on behalf* of the wildebeest."

For a moment, all was quiet except for the soft cracking of the fire. Each member of the group was momentarily lost in his or her own thoughts, suspended under a black canopy sprinkled with stars.

Reflecting on his company meetings, Sean could easily see how important it was to get the "fighting spirit" back into his team. The poor economy had caused many people to feel the pinch on different levels—something that brought about a fair amount of stress and a loss of focus. Many of his team members were at the office in body, but not in spirit. Sean wanted everyone to feel as though they were in this together—to do so, they needed a more defined common goal and commitment to support each other through these tough times. If his team could only visualize the many threats and struggles the wildebeest endured, perhaps their hardships wouldn't seem so insurmountable.

Abruptly, a pack of hyenas started howling not too far away.

"Well, I hate to break the spell, but now it's *really* time for us seniors to turn in," Dave remarked.

Everyone stood up, wished each other a good night's rest, and started down the path to their tents.

"Remember," Anthony said, "Raymond leaves sharply at seven in the morning. We'll meet you in front of the mess tent at six for breakfast. Sean and Ashley—don't forget to dress warmly, bring a hat, sunscreen, and your cameras."

Walking back toward their tent, Ashley nestled close to Sean to ward off the bite in the air. "Sean, how come you never mentioned Zachariah before?"

"Well, I never thought of him much after university. He was just someone I went to school with. He helped me along the way, but there were many interesting people from all over the world. I suppose I never thought I'd see him again."

"Well, he's a very eloquent speaker. And his voice is so melodic and soothing. Are you happy you came now?"

37

"Yes, dear," Sean said, as he smiled crookedly at her. Although it was certainly a loaded question, he had to admit that the day had definitely ended better than it had begun.

Back at their tent there was a lamp burning. Once again, two bowls of hot water and fresh towels were on the table, along with chocolates on their pillows.

Sean looked at Ashley as he flopped on the bed.

"I was just wondering, what if we didn't go with Raymond and the others tomorrow?"

"I don't understand."

"Well, this safari is supposed to be about seeing wildlife—and the concept Zachariah introduced of learning key survival skills from animals adds a whole different dimension to the trip. What if we get up early and ask if we can join him instead?"

Ashley put her towel down and sat on the edge of the bed. "Do you think he'd let us?"

"Why not? Chatting with him and learning about the skills while seeing the animals will be infinitely more stimulating. And we'll promise to stay out of the way when he has to work."

"Spending the whole day hearing his insights *would* be special," Ashley smiled. "So what do we do? Are you going to go ask him now?"

"No. He said he was leaving at four. How about we get there before that and invite ourselves along?"

With that thought they turned off the gas lamp. The moon had climbed high in the sky and was shining brightly through the mosquito netting. The hyenas howling in the distance were now joined by a pack of wild dogs.

SKILL 1: ENDURANCE

Summary

Like the wildebeest, *Endurance*—in its simplest form—is our ability to apply ourselves for relatively long periods of time. It keeps our minds going when our bodies want to quit, and gives us the mental capability to continue moving forward despite the obstacles, hardships, pain, fatigue, or stress in our path.

People often reference the ability to endure as "weathering the storms of life." It's not whether we encounter them in the first place, but rather how we face and handle them that makes the difference. These storms can alter the course of life; the way we prepare to cope with them has a great impact on how we survive them, and whether we emerge from the experience stronger for having endured them.

Every professional ordeal or personal hardship we encounter is an opportunity to hone this skill—which you might recognize in yourself if you exhibit the following characteristics:

- You have resilience and the ability to bounce back from adversity.
- You are adept at changing conditions and pressures from multiple directions. You see problems as challenging rather than discouraging and as opportunities rather than setbacks.
- You are an individual with a competitive edge and are always willing to invest the time and effort required to accomplish tasks.
- You remain focused on established goals and plans in the midst of difficult situations. Every project represents your best effort regardless of its struggles.
- You have worked through the challenges you've experienced with stamina, tenacity, and confidence. Others

consider you to be an exceptionally diligent and hard worker.

Maximizing This Skill

Whether it comes naturally or you need to work at it, tenacity is vital to achieving success. The actions below will help you improve your personal endurance capabilities:

- Take care of your physical needs and build your mental endurance by actively challenging your brain in difficult situations throughout the day—especially when you're tempted to be mentally weak. Avoid escapism, the emotional uncertainty that says, "I can't do anything about it."
- Focus on discriminating between what is important and what isn't, and direct your efforts and resources accordingly. The key here is to establish realistic goals and take steps toward reaching them by asking yourself: what can I achieve today?
- View problems with a long-term perspective, and focus on what you *can* accomplish versus what you can't. Accept the fact that some circumstances are beyond your control, and while you may not be able to change some events, you do control the way you interpret and react to them.

- Remain flexible and patient while keeping things in perspective in order to take appropriate action. Hone your ability to quickly adapt and stay the course even when the going gets tough.
- Develop mutually supportive and caring relationships at home and at work to enhance your ability to persist through challenging situations. There is strength in numbers.

Remember that anything worth having, any challenge worth achieving, or any goal worth reaching will require endurance.

Chapter 3

THE STRATEGIC LION

S ean jumped upright in his bed to the sound of a lion's roar that seemed as though it was right next to him. It felt as if he had just closed his eyes only a moment ago. It was still very dark outside. Then he saw Ashley getting dressed among the dancing shadows attached to the lamp's flickering light.

"Did you hear that?"

"Sure did, honey. Your personalized wake up call."

"Funny."

"Time to get up! It's 3:45, and we need to get going if we want to catch Zachariah before he leaves at 4:00."

As they ran toward the mess tent the smell of wood smoke was drifting through the camp. A kettle was already heating water for morning coffee.

Ashley bent down to warm her hands over the fire and stared at the old enamel pot that was coated black from a thousand campfires. Its wooden handle had the tooth marks of some nighttime visitor that had long ago tried to steal it, only to find its contents too hot to handle.

"Ash, did you get any sleep last night? I just laid there looking at the stars through the mesh and listening to all those wild sounds. I must have drifted off because that roar really woke me this morning," Sean said.

Just then Aly stepped out of the mess tent.

"Mr. and Mrs. Spencer, what are you doing up so early? You only need to be here at six for breakfast."

"We're hoping to catch a ride with Zachariah," replied Sean.

"Zach? You can't do that. Raymond is your guide."

"I understand, but I'd love to spend the day discussing old times with him, and I may not get another chance."

"I see. Well, you'll have to ask him. He has never taken guests with him before, but I suppose you're different."

"Ask me what?" Zachariah said, strolling into the light with two green safari knapsacks, one over each shoulder.

"Ah, Zachariah, good morning."

"Morning Sean, Ashley. A tad early for you two Californians, isn't it?"

"Not if we're joining you on your excursion to the Grumeti River."

"Oh. I'm not sure you want to do that," Zachariah responded. "It's a very long and rough drive, probably three or four hours. My Jeep isn't as nice as Raymond's Land Rover; I've got an open top, and the ride will be hot and dusty."

"That's okay. After last night, we really would love to spend more time with you, and have a chance to see Africa from your perspective. We are intrigued by the different animal skills you spoke about."

"Well, honestly, I'd really enjoy your company; that is, as long as it's okay with Aly."

Aly was standing at the entrance of the dining tent, frowning. "Are you sure you want to go with Zach? Your trip has already been planned with Raymond, and the Land Rover is outfitted with comfortable high view seats. We made a great breakfast and lunch and have plenty of cold water and drinks for the day."

"Please, Aly," Ashley pleaded.

"Well, alright, but before you leave with Zachariah I will need you to sign a release form."

"Release form?" Sean asked with concern.

"To release us from anything that may happen to you today while you are no longer under our protection."

"What could happen?"

"You are in the African bush, Mr. Spencer. This is the wild. *Anything* can happen."

"We'll be fine, honey," Ashley chimed in. "It's just paper-work. The same stuff is printed on the back of your ticket when you go to any theme park. I'm sure Zachariah will take good care of us."

After they had signed the waivers, Zachariah led them to his Jeep. Sean tossed their day bag in the back with Zachariah's equipment bag, while Aly transferred a food container across from the Land Rover. "Enjoy your day and we will see you for a sundowner when you return."

Zachariah slid behind the wheel and immediately headed northwest toward the Grumeti River. Sean and Ashley were still sleepy so they rode in silence until the horizon began to lighten behind them. It was still a bit chilly, and Ashley was glad she'd brought her sweater along. As if reading her mind, Zachariah spoke up for the first time since leaving camp. "It won't be long until the sun gets up over the skyline and things warm up. You will be surprised at how fast it heats up—just as quickly as it got cold last night."

They had rounded a long bend when Zachariah pointed off to their right toward a group of trees. "See those birds over there, just lifting out of that big acacia tree? Those are vultures—some of the first creatures to get going in the morning. They're part of Africa's cleanup crew, and they're conducting an airborne search for whatever might be left over from last night. Not much gets wasted out here."

"We were intrigued with your discussion of the wildebeest last night," Sean said. "I thought about them while listening to all the strange sounds of the night."

"Yes," Ashley said. "There's a part of me that feels sorry for the wildebeest. It seems as if their entire lives are just one step from death."

"Understandably so, but don't feel too badly, Ashley. Each animal has a role to play in nature's overall balancing act. The strongest members of each species succeed and guarantee the survival of the species as a whole. That's what is so amazing about the Serengeti; nature's plan is all clearly laid out for us to observe and learn.

"Let me see if I can couch this in everyday 'American' terms. Remember how the disintegration of the subprime mortgage market led to the collapse of banks, investment institutions, insurance companies, and then automobile manufacturers? The same kind of domino effect applies to nature. If the wildebeest doesn't migrate, then many other animals like the lion, cheetah, and hyena—and even the environment itself—are impacted."

Suddenly, Zachariah brought the Jeep to a stop under a large tree. "Lion tracks!" he called out, pointing at a fresh lion spoor leading toward a group of bushes not more than 30 yards away.

At that moment, five lionesses emerged followed by four cubs, biting at each other's ears and tails. After taking a few steps, they slowly laid down on the perimeter of the bushes, licking their paws and washing their faces. The lionesses looked at the Jeep with idle curiosity and without apparent aggression.

Ashley could hardly breathe as she watched the cubs move toward the female lions. Zachariah spoke softly, "I know this pride; what you see here are the aunts and the cubs. We'll just wait here for a bit; the hunting lionesses and male are no doubt out in the bush somewhere."

The sunlight was just beginning to reach the valley floor and only a few portions of the bush remained gray under the gradually brightening sky. The lions' activities continued with the usual socializing and grooming when suddenly, three large lionesses emerged from the bushes, their bodies swaying with easy power—bringing the total number of lions to twelve. From the opposite direction, an adult lion with a huge mane walked into sight. He seemed to be staring straight at them, and as if on cue, every lioness did the same.

Zachariah looked over his shoulder. "That's what the old boy is looking at."

They followed his gaze and saw about 20 zebras feeding in an area of short grass just on the other side of the tall grass, apparently oblivious to the danger now only a short 100 yards away.

"Don't they know the lions are here?" whispered Ashley, almost afraid to utter a sound with the lionesses now all standing. None of them moved so much as a tail. Even the cubs were hunkered down in the tall grass as if by some silent command.

"They're downwind, and the zebras haven't seen or heard the lions yet. Get your camera ready, Ashley. You are about to witness one of nature's greatest learning experiences firsthand."

The lionesses crept slowly along the edge of the bushes toward a small group of trees on the perimeter of the clearing where the zebras were feeding. Two younger lionesses stayed with the cubs, which were still lying in the tall grass like little statues. It was difficult to see the lionesses as they crouched down and slowly edged toward the browsing herd.

Suddenly, the herd scattered in every direction; one of them had spotted something. A few made a dash while looking around and trying to figure out where the danger was. They regrouped and came to a standstill, this time with an old mare standing a little apart from the herd. Heads were turning and tails were twitching, swishing away the flies; but otherwise, everything seemed peaceful. One of the zebras looked in the direction of the lions. At that very moment all the lions froze in their tracks. A moment later the zebras put their heads down to graze again.

"During the energy-sapping 100 degrees of the summer sun the lion pride will usually remain inactive in whatever shade they can find. That's why they are hunting in the morning when it's cooler, and they can take full advantage of the dawn's lower light conditions."

After what seemed like an eternity of peaceful har-
mony, the lionesses fanned out ever so slowly, advancing toward the herd inch by inch. They glided silently
through the bush in complete unison, emulating the
actions of the lead lioness. It was clear that she had singled out the old mare that had strayed from the herd.

Ashley looked back at the male, who had barely moved
from where he first appeared. The zebras turned and
slowly began to move in the opposite direction. Once
they were in place, the other lionesses began once
again stalking slowly forward, moving from bush to
grass clump. The pride slowly worked its way toward
its target.

Then, the male lion abruptly roared, emitting an explo-
sive bellow that clearly commanded authority. Zachariah
nodded toward him, "I don't believe that there are many
more impressive sights than one's first glimpse of a big
maned lion, free and in charge of his own territory." The
zebras lifted their heads, sounding the alarm and bolting
away in the opposite direction. The old mare was a split
second too slow, and the lead lioness buried her claws
in her shoulder—forcing both down into the tall grass.
Within seconds, two other lions were there to ensure
their meal stayed put. By now, the rest of the zebras
were looking down from the top of a slight rise about
100 yards away.

Sean and Ashley remained in the Jeep, completely in awe of what they just experienced. Then a tawny blur flashed within a few yards of the Jeep. The male approached the lionesses and as he neared them he rushed forward, snarling and scattering them. He clamped his paws on the zebra and began immediately to feed as the females watched.

"I don't think I have ever seen anything so violent, yet so amazing," Sean said, without taking his eyes off the lions.

"It's all about survival," Zachariah responded.

No one spoke as they watched act two unfold in front of them. After feeding, the male went to lie down under a tree. By that time, the lionesses had fetched the cubs they had left in a safe spot before the hunt—and all joined in for their share.

"Consider yourselves very fortunate. It's very rare that anyone gets to witness a lion kill on their first day on safari; in fact, most people never do. In all the years I've been out here, I've only seen it this close a half dozen times. We'd best move on now; we have a deadline to make at the Grumeti."

The three were soon enjoying breakfast as they rambled through the savannahs under the rapidly climbing sun in the African sky. The bush was starting to grow on him, Sean thought. His daily office challenges now seemed like a distant memory.

"What are you thinking about, Sean?" Zachariah asked.

Sean pondered a moment as he let the last few drops of an ice cold drink quench his dry throat. "I was amazed at how all the lionesses moved forward as a single unit, despite the fact that they couldn't even see each other most of the time. Then, when the herd started to move, they readjusted their ranks and didn't attack until their leader gave the signal."

"It was incredible," Ashley chimed in. "Now I follow what you meant last night when you said that we needed to experience the animals first before trying to understand their primary skill. So—what skill do we learn from the lion?"

"Well, there is always one lioness within their hierarchy that leads the hunt as the primary provider for the pride," Zachariah replied.

"Was that the one that moved out to the side in front of all the others?"

"Yes, she set the whole attack plan in motion. If you noticed, no one moved until she did—not even the male."

"Who would have thought," Sean wondered out loud. "Everyone always talks about the king of the jungle, not the queen! Have we had it wrong this whole time?"

"No, the male is still the king of the jungle. You saw what happened after the kill; he made it very clear to all concerned that *he* was going to feed first. That said, the lionesses are still the ultimate predators in the lion family. Each one has her particular role and develops specific skills as part of the well-designed plan. The hunt was precisely set up and tactically executed with skill, precision, and teamwork."

"It certainly was as impressive an operation as I have ever seen."

"During the rainy season, the lions pretty much have it all their own way. Pride territories are less than 10 square miles and food is plentiful most of the time, especially at the height of the calving season. Sometimes they will gorge themselves, consuming more than 50 pounds of meat at a time—roughly four times what they normally eat in one day."

As you saw, the hunt began when the lead lioness singled out the old mare. Each female knew what her role was when the stalk started. At the same time, you saw how they relied on each other and their stealth to get close."

"Why did they wait to get so close before going on the attack? Weren't they worried they would scare the zebras away?" Ashley asked.

"Zebras can outrun a lion over longer distances, especially beyond 100 yards. Stretching the chase beyond that increases their chance of getting away with each additional yard. To prevent that from happening, the lions' plan incorporates a number of key elements.

You saw how they skillfully used every bit of vegetation as cover and maneuvered to remain in the tall grass as long as possible, while at the same time ensuring that they were always downwind from the herd. One whiff and the whole bunch would have been off and running. If they execute these elements correctly, the odds of surprising their prey are in their favor."

"So lions have to *plan* to have breakfast?" Sean quizzed Zachariah.

"Yes, and they do so down to every move. The initial execution is slow and calculating, but the actual attack itself is short and fast. When that lioness made her move she probably accelerated up to 40 miles per hour, a speed she could have kept up for 100 yards or so. It is the unexpected and swift execution that allows the lioness to catch her prey off guard. By the time the zebra realized that the lioness was there, it was already too late. Failure to react for even a split second is often the difference between life and death."

Sean was amazed. "I didn't realize that lions strategically planned out every attack in so much detail—a whole series of steps and key moves. I just assumed that they could eat what they want when they wanted it."

"Assumptions are often dangerous, Sean; you know that. And on the Serengeti, there is no room for error. That's why these skills are so starkly accentuated here—and why we can recognize and relate to them more easily."

Sean thought for a moment.

"I can see how vital it is for the lion to think strategically. As the head of my company, I—more than anyone— can appreciate the importance of planning in this way. But are you saying that every activity *needs* to be done in a strategic matter, the entire time?"

"Well, strategy is much more than a once-a-year ritual. Business leaders need to reduce the overall strategy down to its smaller bit size components."

"So the lion shows us how important strategy is to our daily activities?"

> *"Strategy is the road map you need to define and achieve your goals."*

"Yes, but it's more than simply having a strategy. It requires that you adopt a strategic mind-set irrespective of who and what you are. The lions show us that, although they are the most dominant and feared predators in the Serengeti ecosystem, there are many other rivals challenging them for the top spot."

"Interesting. So even the king of the jungle has competitors."

"Absolutely; everyone does—lions, individuals, and companies. And before any of us embark on any project—whether growing a company or going to university—we always create a detailed set of blueprints to show us the way. Success is seldom an accidentally discovered treasure; rather, it's the result of following a predetermined set of steps by utilizing a combination of various skills.

"Just like the lions worked together to chase down that zebra, each team member has a part to play in the overall plan. If the lion's hunt is unsuccessful, the pride goes hungry. If everyone on your team doesn't understand and work on the plan together, your company may fail.

59

"As the leader of your company, you need to work with each team member to help them understand how their individual actions impact the desired outcome of overall strategy."

Shaking his head, Sean grinned. "I wonder how many people on my team have even bothered to read the company business plan thoroughly."

"Well, think about what we just saw. Isn't it evident that every lion understands its role in the overall strategy?"

"Oh, sure. But I'd be surprised if there are even a handful of companies where everyone is on the same page. And plans change the whole time."

"Remember the lead lioness; she developed the strategy and resulting plan of attack. But when the herd began to move off, she made an adjustment."

A light breeze came up as Zachariah steered the Jeep off the narrow road into the short, dry, grass plains.

"You see, Sean," Zachariah continued, "Planning includes considering alternatives and options. The difficulty lies in the fact that each one of our choices contains a new array of thoughts, expectations, ideas, and perceptions.

Consequently, the outcome of each choice creates a new set of options and obstacles. Therefore, each decision impacts the next, and so on. So it's critical to ensure that you are on the right track—or all your choices could end up being worthless."

"Well, that certainly makes sense. So, what tips might you have for your old college buddy's business?" Sean asked teasingly.

"The first thing you need to do is to make sure that all your team members understand the vision you have for the company. Second, you must encourage them all to participate in creating the company's strategy to get there."

Zachariah paused for a moment. "Third, you need to empower team members to determine the action plans they require to implement their part of the strategy successfully."

"Agreed. And I know we learned that at business school—but it's challenging to put all of that into operation," Sean sneered.

"Well, sure, but you want to be king of the jungle, right?" Zachariah shot back quickly. "Remember, each of the lionesses knew what the goal was and what her role was in achieving it."

"Yes, but isn't business a bit more complex than hunting?" Sean countered.

"Is it? Maybe, maybe not. However, it doesn't really matter; we're not comparing. Rather, we're learning. The lion's unique survival skill illustrates the importance of being strategic in every action you take. And if lions are, shouldn't you?"

Sean thoroughly enjoyed this exchange of ideas—and he was amazed. Here he was, 10,000 miles from California, in the middle of the bush, having an excellent and insightful discussion on business strategies. Sean had always had a strong loyalty toward his team and a very committed work ethic. But as CEO, he had few peers with whom he could share his concerns or problems. In addition, his company's declining revenues had forced him to change his management style to that of crisis control rather than visionary leadership. He knew that he needed to fix that. Sean promised himself that as soon as he was back, he was going to update his team's plan, get every member onboard and focused, and hold everyone—including himself—more accountable.

"Zachariah, while you and Sean were talking, a question came to mind," Ashley said. "I was thinking about how much more a family would accomplish if they were as strategic as those lions were. I'm not exactly sure of what I'm trying to say, but I thought of it last night as well, when you discussed the wildebeests' skill. It seems that both of these skills could also be harnessed into our personal lives."

"Absolutely, Ashley. Although our consulting company is applying the research to business, the skills have a much wider application for families and individuals. For example, we all remember the kid who knew exactly what he wanted to be when he grew up: a professional athlete, an actor, a neurosurgeon, or whatever. He had discovered the strategy skill of the lion within himself at a young age and had it all figured out. However, it usually takes soul searching, hard work, and many years before most other people uncover their strengths or desires. They have to define their dreams and strategize on how they can make those dreams come true—even from an early stage in life."

SKILL 2: STRATEGY

Summary

For lions, it's all or nothing. If their *Strategy* fails, they go hungry. For us, however, it's all about organizing our thoughts, ideas, experiences, skills, expertise, and expectations to accomplish a desired goal.

Strategy is not just about the end; rather, it's the means to that end. For that reason, sound strategies must be flexible, not rigid. In its simplest form it's a basic road map—albeit one that involves and incorporates change. This might make it not only difficult to accurately read at times, but also somewhat dependent on future uncertainty.

HERE ARE SOME THOUGHTS TO PUT IT IN PERSPECTIVE:

- Strategy is the art and science of enabling an organization, team, or individual to achieve its objectives through a series of choices, plans, and actions.
- Strategy requires quick and appropriate responses to shifting conditions.
- Strategy can be difficult to develop when you aren't aware of all the details. Occasionally, we must make a guess based on common sense and the information available at the time.

IF YOU ARE A STRATEGIC PERSON—A STRATEGIST—YOU WILL RECOGNIZE THESE CHARACTERISTICS IN YOURSELF:

- The ability to create multiple options for solving problems.
- You chart the course that others follow by defining the tactics, steps, and resources that are required to

achieve the goal while keeping the bigger picture in perspective. You remain proactive and ensure that the plan is adjusted to meet the objectives.

• Strategic thinkers know that effective planning and execution is a team effort. They're highly collaborative and adept at weaving visions with pragmatic, timely initiatives, and tend to challenge existing assumptions and generate transformations over the short and long term.

Maximizing This Skill

TO TRULY TAP INTO YOUR CORE COMPETENCY AS A STRATEGIC LION, YOU NEED TO KNOW:

• Who you are.
• What you want.
• Where you're going.
• How you will get there.
• What you are going to do once you get there.

It's as simple as that; build a road map and execute the plan.

To create a successful strategy, you must first develop a goal and a written plan to achieve that goal. Always include the following three key elements: (1) **your objectives**—these become milestones to measure over time and provide you checkpoints for success along the way; (2) **the tactics**—the approach you are going to use to achieve the goal, and (3) **the resources**—in the form of your own and others' skills—that you need to affect the plan.

This is your life and your career; make sure you know where you are heading.

Chapter 4

THE ENTERPRISING CROCODILE

After leaving whatever semblance there was of a track behind, Zachariah continued to press deeper into the veldt. Sean watched in amazement as he avoided all the rocks, termite mounds, and holes; he had no idea how Zachariah did it. Few animals looked up as the Jeep passed by and then only with casual curiosity.

It was almost nine when they arrived at the Grumeti River. Zachariah pulled up on a ridge overlooking a major crossing area. They parked in the shade of a large acacia tree with a clear view of the rapidly flowing, murky river. It was a short 200 yards to the thousands of wildebeest milling on the opposite embankment above the river's edge.

"I've never seen that many animals all bunched up together like that!" Ashley exclaimed.

"How many will be crossing today?" Sean asked.

"Well, last year's first crossing had over 20,000 wildebeest. I suspect we'll see close to that number again."

"They really seem uneasy, almost agitated. What's wrong?"

"Look on the opposite side of the river, by that sand-bar to the left, just next to the footpath going up the embankment."

"Alligators!"

"*Nile* crocodiles actually. They're much larger than the American alligator and can grow up to 16 feet in length and weigh an average of 500 pounds. Though most of their diet consists of fish, they'll eat anything that drinks from or crosses the river. Many weak, old, and inexperienced wildebeest will succumb today to these age-old reptiles. But far more will actually drown due to the swift current."

"Wow," Sean said, looking through the binoculars. "You only have to look at these guys up close to realize they're formidable killers."

"The croc has few natural enemies and can live to be 100 years old. The wildebeest migration and the river crossing is their favorite time of the year."

The expanding group of wildebeest now filled the entire landscape on the far side of the river. A number of zebras joined but seemed to be lingering together at the rear of the herd.

"No one ever really knows when they are going to cross the river. The herd will continue to grow and mill around at the river's edge for an indefinite period of time until one wildebeest breaks the spell."

Zachariah motioned just minutes later and announced, "It's time."

What began as one wildebeest quickly became a barrage jumping into the river. The animals mechanically followed each other, pushing against the current in a wide shoulder-to-shoulder line. Sean and Ashley sat stunned at the vast exhibition unfolding before them. It was remarkable for them to actually witness this scene: thousands of wildebeest crossing a raging river while crocodiles patiently waited for the right moment to identify a straggler and swiftly seize the opportunity. In a matter of seconds, a wildebeest was pulled beneath the surface while the other wildebeest pushed forward and up the side of the muddy embankment.

"Although each individual crossing only takes a few minutes, the group's size means that today's crossing will take many hours. For a few this was their last day, but for the vast majority of wildebeest this is but one hurdle in their epic journey—they still have a long road ahead."

"I've always understood that nature is all about the survival of the strongest, but watching it play out right in front of my eyes for the second time this morning gives me a whole new appreciation for it," Sean said.

Ashley stared straight ahead as she spoke, almost to herself. "I'm not sure I understand this. I'm overwhelmed, and honestly, even a little sad."

"You've got to take a step away from what you have just seen, Ashley, to try to gain some perspective," Zachariah said as he began packing up his equipment. "Let's head back and find a nice spot overlooking the savannahs and we'll discuss the skill we just saw."

The sun was near its zenith. Just to cool down, Sean and Ashley were standing and holding onto the Jeep's roll bar while the wind danced through their hair. As the terrain became increasingly difficult to navigate, Zachariah slowed down before pulling in at a shady setting under a tree.

"Lookout points never cease to amaze me. I am always inspired by the expansiveness of Africa," said Zachariah as he went to the back of the Jeep and brought out two old beaten up aluminum folding chairs and the cooler. He passed around some much-needed ice cold drinks.

"Okay, Ashley. Tell me what you experienced earlier," Zachariah prompted.

"The only thing I saw was the wildebeest's struggle to cross the river and avoid being killed by crocodiles or drowning in the gushing water."

"How about you, Sean?"

"I guess I'd have to agree with Ash. It seemed to be a brutal process that just kept repeating itself."

"Interesting. You were both focused on the wildebeest's action."

"Yes, well—I suppose we were . . ."

"I understand. However, the skill we are assessing is demonstrated by the crocodile—so you should turn your attention to their point of view," Zachariah paused.

"Unlike the lion, the crocodile can't chase after his prey; he has to wait for it to come to him. And to make matters even more complicated, all animals sense the crocodile's presence in the water. So the crocodile has to be very stealthy and enterprising to obtain its meal.

"Although the wildebeest migration brings the crocs an abundance of food, it's also dangerous for them, since the crocs could easily be trampled to death by thousands of hooves. They have to identify the stragglers and the weak ones and then seek out the best moment to grab their prey before they get in the way of the next wildebeest crossing the river."

"Are you saying the crocodiles are *enterprising*?" Sean asked, stunned.

"Yes, Sean."

"They look more like opportunists," Sean observed, still surprised.

"Well, the label 'opportunist' has a somewhat negative connotation. Step back for a second and think. What's wrong with taking advantage of an opportunity that presents itself?"

"Well if you frame it that way . . . nothing, I suppose."

"I sat over there many, many days watching the river. For a long time I, too, saw the crocodile in a disapproving way. And then one day it hit me: the crocodiles are not the reason for the migration—they didn't choose the path. It's merely the harshness of reality that makes one side with the wildebeest."

74

> *"An enterprising person explores all options and boldly seizes every opportunity."*

Looking into the distance, Zachariah spoke again. "In some regards the crocodile is the bona fide entrepreneur of this jungle."

"That's certainly a constructive way to view them," Sean replied.

"And that's it, Sean. An opportunist is always looking for a way to gain the advantage, no matter what it takes; they're seeking a means to an end. On the other hand, the enterprising individual positions himself or herself to take advantage of legitimate opportunities that arise *without* exploiting others.

"Sean, I believe that the reason many businesses fail is because they're so wrapped up in daily operations that they don't see the countless available opportunities. That's where this skill helps us refocus. You can usually count on enterprising people to be prepared to act when the occasion presents itself. Many people never see it, many aren't prepared for it, some don't act fast enough—or others just let these possibilities slip through their fingers.

"But the crocodile evaluates every animal that enters his realm as an opportunity. The assessment is done in a very methodical manner and the execution is swift."

"So is this a ruthless business-only skill set?" Ashley asked.

"Oh, no!" exclaimed Zachariah. "This is a hugely important life skill as well. After all, wouldn't you be remiss if you didn't seize an opportunity that would create a better environment or circumstance for your daughters?"

"Of course."

"Remember, it isn't simply 'taking' advantage; it's developing a mind-set to actively *seek* opportunities. Maybe it's a new school, or an educational prospect, or an introduction to someone that could enhance your career—you fill in the blanks. We need to sensitize our mind-set to evaluate every opportunity that comes our way—irrespective of how small—in both our personal and business lives."

"Well . . . not *every* opportunity," Sean said.

"And why not? I said evaluate—not take. You can't afford to leave any stone unturned. Remember, in the Serengeti your life may depend on it."

As he noticed the sun nearing its peak in the sky, Zachariah decided that it was time for them to start heading back to camp, as he still had two stops that he wanted to make on the way back. "Grab another bottle of water; I want to quickly drive down there to the grasslands. There is another survival skill I want to show."

SKILL 3: ENTERPRISING

Summary

Enterprising means showing initiative, a willingness to undertake new projects, and a strong desire for success and achievement—all qualities that support the role of the entrepreneur. Like the crocodile, enterprising people possess the energy, creativity, and ambition required to see the possibilities in the future that others cannot see. Enterprising individuals are passionate about their work, learn from mistakes, understand their weaknesses as well as their strengths, recognize opportunity, and make strategic decisions with limited data.

IF YOU ARE AN ENTERPRISING PERSON, YOU'LL SEE THE FOLLOWING CHARACTERISTICS IN YOURSELF:

- The ability to "think outside the box" when facing difficult problems and developing solutions.

- A dedication to advancing both yourself and your organization through a clear mission, while fostering a culture that supports and encourages imaginative and creative solutions.
- The determination to succeed, which also lends itself to another important trait for enterprising individuals: self-confidence.
- The tendency to spend a lot of time working alone— something that's paramount to business success. This emphasizes entrepreneurs' understanding of sacrifice, and how short-term hard work will pay off with long-term rewards.

Entrepreneurs have a strong desire to lead rather than follow; they seek out opportunities that specifically provide a great deal of autonomy. They seek out change, rather than fearing it.

Maximizing This Skill

Entrepreneurs and enterprising individuals always display a willingness to go against the crowd and stand above. They take advantage of difficult situations and don't allow them to become burdens. As with any skill, there are a number of pitfalls to avoid:

- Failing to evaluate and analyze the potential risks involved and developing a plan to address them early on.

- Failing to constantly communicate with others involved, ensuring that they understand what is required of them, verifying that they have the necessary resources and/or skills, and are empowered and authorized to complete the tasks for which they are being held accountable.

Enterprising people understand exactly what to do when opportunity knocks.

Chapter 5

THE EFFICIENT
CHEETAH

he granite kopjes' rough and jumbled surfaces were formed from years of volcanic activity that had been eroded by the sun and the rain. Navigating straight downhill where there was no pathway was considerably bumpier than the river's landscape.

"Over there!" Zachariah shouted.

Sean picked up the long-range binoculars again and looked in the direction Zachariah was pointing, but there were literally hundreds of mounds. "Which one?" he asked.

"The termite mound right in the middle of the grassland, about 150 yards out."

"What animal are we looking for?"

Just then, a blur of gold flashed from behind the grass and a beautiful cheetah jumped on top of the mound. She sat there carefully scanning a 360-degree circle. No one said a word for what seemed like an eternity. The cheetah appeared to be six to seven feet in length with a round face, a cat's long tail, and long ears. Her chest was deep, and narrowed as it approached her waist. But most striking was her sleek appearance and the beautifully black-spotted tan coat—perfect camouflage for the dry savannah grass.

"Is it male or female?" asked Ashley, as the face in the binoculars seemed to look straight at her.

"She's female, and a mother. She's looking for lunch and checking out those gazelles grazing about 100 yards away to the right."

"She is incredibly beautiful. Sean, look how sleek she looks. Look! There are two little cubs just climbing up. Oh, they're absolutely adorable."

Zachariah put down his binoculars and pointed toward a group of trees in the distance. "Look way back there in the shadows of that acacia tree. See the lions? Their day's work is done; they'll be doing nothing till sunset. Just like the pride we saw earlier, they appear to have fed and will now spend the rest of the day trying to stay out of the heat. The temperature under that tree can be as much as 20 degrees cooler than where the cheetah is.

"This big grassland is perfect open territory, and that termite mound provides a great vantage point. That's why cheetahs favor the open plains. Plus, she generally has the savannahs to herself while the lions and hyenas are sleeping.

"If we wait patiently, I would say there is a fairly good chance we will see her make a move," Zachariah said.

What an eclectic bag of opposites, Sean thought. One moment they witnessed a tormenting river, then a place of tranquility, and then a race for survival. Was his life back in LA the same? A jumbled series of events and a pursuit for continued existence?

The gazelles continued feeding, their tails flipping like little fans—not seeming the least bit concerned about the cheetah staring at them.

"Since the cheetah's two young cubs will take a long time to reach maturity, they are highly dependent on their mother for food and protection for as much as eighteen months after their birth. That's what she's considering right now, studying those gazelles so intently. Now that she realizes *we're* not a threat, she'll make her move."

Suddenly, the cubs stopped playing. They laid down in the grass, seemingly in response to some unheard command from their mother. She dropped down into the long grass and disappeared. As the breeze flowed over the tall grass, her movement went completely unnoticed. Zachariah pointed to a large rock outcropping about 30 yards from the gazelles.

"She's headed for that spot closer to the gazelles. It's downwind, which will allow her to get extremely close. It's more about vision than smell for her; she'll use her eyesight to get close to her target. Since she's a lone hunter, the element of surprise is very important."

They watched as the cheetah emerged from the grass, still barely visible as she crept behind another outcrop, constantly remaining out of sight. She gradually assessed the terrain and the distance to her prey. The world seemed to stop, and they could almost feel her muscles tense for the attack. The gazelles were still oblivious to the impending peril, and it appeared that she had singled out one that had strayed from the group. Rapidly, the cheetah accelerated and attained full speed in seconds, covering 30 yards in the blink of an eye. In less than a minute, she was holding the gazelle by the throat and kept on gripping the neck for about five minutes until it was dead.

As the hot breeze blew the cloud of dust from the chase out onto the plain, the mother cheetah slowly dragged the meal back to her cubs. She continually surveyed all directions looking for anyone who had intentions of stealing her cubs' lunch. Sean and Ashley sat mesmerized as the family ate their meal.

Zachariah broke the silence. "There are very few animals that can survive a chase by a cheetah. There aren't any speed limits here on the Serengeti, and at 70 miles an hour, she is the fastest land predator on the planet. Her small head, slim body, and powerful rangy legs give her the ability to attain that speed. She can also turn instantly without faltering, since her long tail helps her maintain perfect balance."

Sean leaned forward and put his binoculars down and asked curiously, "How long can she keep up that speed?"

"Not very long. She uses a tremendous amount of energy to run at top speed, which causes her body temperature and heart rate to rise rapidly. That's why she's lying there next to her cubs now, panting and not feeding. Expending all that energy in such a short span of time requires her to rest for at least 20 minutes in order to catch her breath and get her body back to normal. That's why she keeps looking around; she's vulnerable to other predators right now. Killing is only half the battle for the cheetah; now she has to defend her prize against others that wouldn't hesitate to steal it while she is recovering. She hunts during the hottest hours of the day because it diminishes the odds that she'll encounter other predators. You might say that she fills a niche that would otherwise be empty; as the saying goes, nature abhors a vacuum."

Sean leaned back and stretched out his legs, the spine-tingling image of a lightning-fast cheetah chasing her prey at 70 miles an hour replaying in his mind. Sean noticed that Ashley couldn't take her eyes off of the cubs that were now feeding while the mother kept watch.

"Americans admire speed, since it's typically associated with winning. Although being fast undeniably has many advantages, its greatest value comes when you temper it with efficiency. Think of it in terms of 'getting the desired result' or 'finishing the job' in the shortest possible time, with minimum wasted resources. Our cheetah mother can't keep that speed up forever—so she certainly doesn't have unlimited resources," Zachariah said.

> *"Efficiency is the optimization of all resources to achieve the best results."*

We humans aren't any different. Our efficiency depends on how well we recognize and respond to both internal and external factors. Things like interruptions, distractions, mistakes, mental and physical fatigue, or lack of experience, or expertise can cause us to lose focus."

"That's quite a list, Zachariah! Are you saying that efficiency always trumps speed?" Sean challenged Zachariah.

"While you undoubtedly have to be ruthless with your time, you cannot do so at the expense of productivity

and effectiveness. The cheetah may be the fastest crea-
ture in the Serengeti, but she also knows that her ability
will be for naught if she loses her prey. She can't afford
to take on a chase that will exhaust her resources before
she can complete the task.

"It's often just the opposite for us. Our unrealistic assumptions can occasionally keep us from making good decisions. We race to meet a deadline, become distracted, lose
focus, consume our resources unwisely, and then complete
the task before the deadline—but with significant errors."

Sean couldn't help but agree. "I've seen a lot of that over
the last couple of years in both our government and my
own company. It's almost become an epidemic in recent
times. We've got lots of room for improvement."

Zachariah walked over to the back of the Jeep, opened
the cool box, and drank half a bottle of water before he
continued. "Efficiency is the ability to accomplish a task
completely and correctly in the least amount of time
and work, while consuming the minimum amount of
resources in the process. For that reason, a team—such
as yours, Sean—simply can't be as effective when they
constantly work at high speed."

"That's certainly true, but with the constant deadlines
we face it's a lot easier said than done."

"I agree. It always is. Speed and efficiency are separate elements, but when properly blended they are an unstoppable combination. Finding that balance is the challenge.

"Sort of like the cheetah out there," Zachariah continued. "If she had chased a different gazelle every few seconds she most likely would not have caught any of them."

"Right," Ashley responded. "The school district I worked for wasn't focused either. They kept chasing multiple objectives. We usually didn't complete projects on time or within budget because of that."

"The first thing you have to do is to identify which practices within an organization are inefficient and replace them with effective practices," Zachariah explained. "Then, you can incorporate the new methods into the everyday workplace to change your team's thought processes and work habits."

"You're already pretty good at managing your time, Sean," Ashley observed.

Sean thought about his daily habits. It was true. He was a firm believer in working smarter, not harder. He liked to use checklists, the latest technology to manage workflow, and he generally leveraged resources to their maximum ability. But he had allowed the company to fall victim to daily deadlines. There was a lot of truth to what Zachariah was saying. Having a plan, staying the course, seizing the opportunity, being efficient—all of these survival skills were required to succeed in the real world as well. While he knew that, he also knew he wasn't doing it anymore. The real lesson for him today included a trip back to basics.

"Now, before you become too concerned about improving the company's efficiency, let me expand your thinking by exposing you to one of the most unique skills the Serengeti has to teach us," Zachariah said.

"What's that?" Sean asked.

"Well, it's a very important skill for everyone to have, but is especially vital in a leader. In fact, it is overlooked more than any other skill."

"What's that?" Ashley asked.

"Hang in there. Keep in mind that you need to experience each animal in its natural habitat first. Let's get back in the Jeep and head toward that tree line so I can show you."

SKILL 4: EFFICIENCY

Summary

Similar to the cheetah, *Efficiency* is all about finishing the job in the shortest possible time with a minimum amount of wasted energy and resources.

IF YOU ARE EFFICIENT, YOU WILL NOTICE THE FOLLOWING HABITS AND QUALITIES IN YOURSELF:

- You search for the most efficient way to achieve a goal without wasting energy by adapting to varying situations, responding to them, and recognizing the factors that affect efficiency.
- You try to avoid excess consumption of resources by recognizing the personal limits that waste them.
- You schedule your day, prioritize every task, and keep those priorities by refining to-do lists frequently and adopting a policy of strict time management. You "chunk" or break your larger projects down into small, easier-to-manage steps.
- You're an effective time manager with the ability to evaluate and deal with those things that get in the way of achieving your goal, such as self-generated interruptions.
- You maintain an orderly "start up/shut down" routine at the beginning and end of each day to help you remain focused and utilize peak times more efficiently.

- You recognize that time is your most precious, and yet most limited, resource. You can't buy more of it, and therefore, how efficiently you use it shapes and affects your life.

Maximizing This Skill

Know your own limits; keep physically healthy and maintain a positive mental attitude. After all, the key to efficiency is to complete the job or task on time and successfully, without putting a strain on the rest of your life.

TO ACCOMPLISH THIS, YOU MUST CONSTANTLY BE ON THE LOOKOUT FOR "INEFFICIENCY" IN THE PROJECT PROCESS, OR YOURSELF, BY:

- Controlling personal sources of friction, such as interruptions and distractions (email, texts, phone calls, web surfing, and so on).
- Continually focus on the process; doing the right thing at the right time.

PERHAPS MOST IMPORTANT, YOU MUST ADOPT A PROACTIVE ATTITUDE BY TAKING THE FOLLOWING ACTIONS:

- Avoid multitasking, and learn to say no.
- Delegate tasks to others where appropriate.

- Look for ways to improve systems and processes—what people do and how they do it—and improve productivity by focusing on getting things done correctly the first time instead of just getting them done cheaply and quickly.
- Ensure that resources—such as personnel and material—are being effectively utilized.

The goal is to get the same results with less input or better results with the same input.

Chapter 6

THE GRACEFUL GIRAFFE

There are few more striking symbols of Africa than the acacia tree. "This is about as far as we can go," Zachariah said, pulling the Jeep up under the gnarled branches of an Umbrella Thorn acacia tree. "We'll walk the last stretch."

"But this is the wild," Ashley protested. "We just saw a cheetah kill a gazelle!"

"Don't worry Ashley. I promised Aly I would keep you safe, didn't I?"

Still feeling a bit apprehensive and not knowing what to expect, Sean and Ashley followed Zachariah closely through the bush. They carefully avoided the thorn bushes' unique weapons: hundreds of little hooks that can grab quickly onto clothing. They walked up a slight crest, and rounding a large thicket they found themselves on the edge of a clearing overlooking a ravine.

There before their eyes, on the opposite ridge, was one of the most beautiful sights imaginable—a herd of giraffes silhouetted against the skyline, meandering between the trees. Nine adult giraffes and three calves were slowly browsing from one treetop to the next.

"There is nothing like seeing a giraffe in its natural habitat. Like the cheetah, giraffes also favor specific places in the Serengeti; they don't join the wildebeest on their annual pilgrimage. Giraffes have a very high tolerance for drought, because they can store an exceptionally large amount of water," Zachariah said.

"Their towering height is so impressive. It's a long way to the top of those trees, yet they seem to soar comfortably above them. How tall do they get?" Sean inquired.

"Well, as the tallest land animals on the planet, they average 14 to 17 feet in height. The long thorns of the acacia tree prevent most animals from eating the leaves, but not the giraffes; they simply use their 18-inch-long tongues to reach around the thorns. They generally spend most of their day eating, as it takes them that long to get full."

"Eating the whole day sounds like fun," Ashley responded.

Sean and Zachariah laughed.

"Do they make any sounds?" Ashley wondered.

"They're very congenial and quiet animals, but they do communicate with coughing or barking sounds. The species we have here on the Serengeti are called the Masai or Kilimanjaro giraffe. Those over there are females with their one-year-old calves. The young males tend to live in bachelor herds, while mature males generally lead solitary lives."

"Aren't they afraid of predators?" Sean asked, thinking again about the cheetah he had just seen.

"Not really. Giraffes can be a very difficult and dangerous choice of prey; one well-placed kick can shatter a predator's skull or break its spine. Lions are the only ones that really pose a serious threat to an adult giraffe. However, once they get galloping they are very tough to stop.

"And they aren't called the 'Watchtowers of the Serengeti' without good reason. Their height gives them ample warning of approaching predators; that's why many other animals like to remain close to them. Here's another fascinating fact—they sleep less than two hours a day."

"Wow! Think of all the additional work I could get done if I only slept for two hours. So, is their skill the ability to maximize time?" Sean asked.

"No, it's not. They may be awake 22 hours a day, but that time isn't really productive."

"Look, Sean," Ashley said enthusiastically. "See those two wandering over there? What a beautiful, rhythmical movement."

"In contrast to other hoofed animals, the giraffe walks by simultaneously moving the left front and right rear legs and then the right front and left rear legs—which causes their bodies and necks to swing gracefully side-to-side."

"Can they can run fast?"

"Yes," Zachariah said. "An adult can easily reach a speed of around 40 miles per hour. It's incredible, don't you think? The tallest mammal in the world is also the most elegant. But, of course, it's more than just their movement. Their sociable behavior also reinforces their role as the most gracious of all animals on the Serengeti. It reinforces that beauty, elegance, and style comes in all sizes."

"That's their skill—grace!" Ashley exclaimed excitedly.

"Very perceptive, Ashley. For most, faith is spiritual—for others it's rational. Most of us believe that the sun will rise tomorrow and that we will wake up healthy. We generally trust that a new day will bring new opportunities. The problem is that many expect them but won't seek them out. Most want them but few will truly appreciate them. A lot of people can only be positive when all is going their way. But that's when it's easy to have an optimistic outlook. The survival skill of grace emphasizes the fact that we must be grateful, even when things aren't going our way," Zachariah said.

Ashley instantly related to this skill, and shared various personal experiences after being let go as a teacher.

"I've seen the dark side of people when things go wrong. When the school district gave pink slips to a group of us last year, none were happy, of course, but everyone reacted differently. Many handled the situation very professionally, others were bad-mouthing the government, while some even started backstabbing their colleagues. The whole situation became nasty and distasteful."

> *"Grace is more than style and finesse, it's doing the right thing."*

"I can imagine," Zachariah responded. "Losing a job is one of the most stressful events a person can encounter. But losing control and respect for your colleagues and reacting in a hurtful and distasteful manner is never the right way.

"Grace teaches us to have patience, patience produces understanding, understanding results in acceptance, and acceptance allows us to move past the stressful situation at hand."

"That's what I tried to do—move past what happened," Ashley said. "I explored a new career outside my field of expertise and my comfort zone. It was very hard at first, and I was definitely scared."

"As one door closes, you must explore all the other doors, both open and closed. The key was that you remained positive," Zachariah said. "Grace is the golden thread that allows us to keep our lives in balance. It can often serve as our purpose and motivation. It helps us with our relationships—which we all know are one of the most difficult things to manage.

"Grace is expressed through so many different qualities: compassion, benevolence, goodness, and generosity. It is a key ingredient in determining how competently we interact with others. That's why it's so important to be gracious not only toward those we love and care about—but also the people who come into our lives every day.

"Your standing in life doesn't matter. The important thing is whether or not you appreciate what you have;

that mind-set will have a profound effect on your attitude. We woke up this morning, enjoyed breakfast, and decided how we were going to spend our day. That makes us more blessed than 95 percent of all the people in the world! For hundreds of millions of people in Africa and other developing countries, just meeting basic needs is a daily struggle."

The giraffes had moved from the cover of the trees into the open savannah and were now completely dominating the landscape.

"The giraffe's grace is embodied in how they move and flow when they run," Zachariah added.

"Being graceful doesn't seem to fit into the business world as obviously as the other skills you've already explained to us. Is it as essential in business as it is in life?" Sean speculated.

"Absolutely. Grace is *imperative* in business. It's how our company interacts with our customers, competitors, suppliers, and even those within our own team. It's so much more than style, finesse, and good taste; it's about doing the right thing, even if it's not required. This skill must be embedded in the very fiber of who we are, what we believe, our appreciation, and the contributions we are willing to make.

"What we do and how we do it reflects our expertise, experience, and values. Winning is important, but how you go about winning is far more important. Your actions must personify dignity, honor, and grace. It can range from not cutting corners and providing the customer with quality service to doing the right thing and always keeping your word. Grace should be central to any business. Some people understand it better if we refer to *grace* as *professionalism*."

"Yes," Sean responded, "I see it better now. It is very important for a company to have a moral compass that can permeate throughout the entire organization."

"And," Ashley chipped in, "it can also help transcend the day-to-day turmoil, allowing people to take a 'longer view' approach."

"Well, just listen to you two! You're both beginning to embrace and connect with the wisdom and meaning, not just the actual skill, of each animal you have observed."

"Oh, but we have such a remarkable teacher," Ashley said, smiling.

Zachariah blushed, and then continued.

"Grace is a key foundation of any form of success. Those who exhibit a true kindness and extend graciousness to others—even when things have not gone their way—are always able to rise above the petty events.

"Why don't you two relax here and continue to enjoy the view for a minute while I go get the Jeep?"

"Are we safe? How close are the lions?" Ashley asked, concerned.

"Ashley, be aware of your surroundings. Look and listen. The giraffes over there on the savannahs are your watchtowers and the zebras in the ravine are your ears. Plus, the large family of guinea fowl in the grass just to our right would have warned us a long time ago if danger was in the vicinity. You're perfectly safe. The lions are still enjoying their afternoon nap," Zachariah said, as he disappeared behind a fig tree.

"Grace. Who would have ever thought?" Sean remarked, as they found a flat spot on an outcrop of vulcanized stone to sit on.

"It's a perfect metaphor for such a beautiful animal. They seem to just tower above it all. Zachariah is an excellent mentor. Not only does he have limitless knowledge of nature and animals, but his understanding and analysis is very unique."

"How do you think I could apply grace to the work, Ash?" Sean wondered.

"Well, you can create a less stressful work environment by removing some of the deadlines. You could try to keep corporate politics from taking root, and maybe design a fun activity your team can do together to motivate them again, as you did when you started the company. Even with the difficult times we're experiencing, we need to remember what Zachariah said: We have it better than most. We need to see how we can help all of your company's employees—especially those that are struggling to make ends meet. Maybe we can create a support group for the spouses, help some of them find a second job if they need one, or even create an educational fund for the kids."

"Wow!" Sean said. "Where did that suddenly come from? Those are all great ideas. Now I remember why I married you."

Ashley smiled. "I'm always looking out for you. You've just been so overworked and too busy to notice recently."

Suddenly, a flock of dark gray birds resembling partridges fluttered noisily up from nowhere and disappeared over the safety of the edge of the ravine.

"What was that?" Ashley said, as she moved closer to Sean.

"Must be the guinea fowl Zachariah mentioned."

"That means something's coming, Sean."

With that, the Jeep broke though the grass and Zachariah pulled up next to them.

"You scared the daylights out of us when the guinea fowl flew up," Sean said.

"Sorry, guys; I didn't mean to. They're always so noisy when they hear anything approaching."

"Zachariah, today's journey has made me realize something. I hate to admit it, but I am often pressed for time, and easily get caught up in the rush of daily activities. That's when I start taking for granted the things that are most important to me—like Ashley," Sean said with a smile. "Connecting with you and having time to experience the animals has really allowed me the opportunity to do a lot of introspection and put my thoughts in perspective. I have to say, though, that I'm also a bit overwhelmed."

"Not to worry, Sean," Zachariah said. "This is only your second day in Africa and you have already experienced so much. Remember for me it's been a life-long journey."

Sean and Ashley took one last look at the giraffes as Zachariah headed back to the dirt road. It was a picture that would come back into their minds on many occasions in the future.

And that in itself was indeed a graceful thought.

SKILL 5: GRACE

Summary

The word *Grace* tends to vary in meaning from one person or situation to another, often depending upon the context in which it is used. While many see the grace of the giraffe in human-like terms such as elegance, charm, or a positive attitude, others consider it to be divine in origin. They believe that it represents that indispensable gift for the development, improvement, and expansion of one's character.

No matter how you see it, grace is a disposition that requires compassion toward others and the desire to extend goodwill. It incorporates the exercise of love and kindness—most important, to those who may not have earned it. Grace is as crucial in business as it is in life.

This truth is embedded in the fiber of who we are, what we believe, our appreciation, and the contribution we make to the world. Gracious people exhibit the following characteristics:

- They seek to make others feel like they're one of the most important people with whom they can spend time, and always put the needs of others first.
- They live according to a personal code that is higher than normal standards of conduct, and incorporate dignity, honor, and respect in extending grace to others—even when things have not gone their way.

Whether it's in our job or in personal matters, grace creates a richer and more fulfilling life. It's not just a skill that some people have and others do not; rather a state of mind acquired by observation and commitment. It is first and foremost a skill that is centered on others— how we treat them and how we put their needs above our own without any consideration or expectation of a return in kind.

Our ability to develop grace isn't based on what we have or don't have. What matters in terms of grace is whether or not we appreciate what we do have, and how we interact with those around us.

Maximizing This Skill

The tone and approach you use with others impacts how you establish grace in your life. It is visible through your language, attitude, and body movements—all of which express your true intent to others.

These qualities are acquired through a personal commitment to focus on changing your attitude toward others. They are evidenced in the workplace by changing:

- Control to coaching
- Managing to mentoring
- Employing to empowering

Graceful individuals develop interdependent relationships that are fostered through patience, self-discipline, dignity, honor, and respect. They accomplish this by recognizing others' strengths and weaknesses, and attempting to build them up. They realize how vital it is to nurture others without expecting recognition for it.

Grace represents style, finesse, kindness, and above all, doing the right thing—a quality that will always advance purpose in life, no matter what it is.

Chapter 7

THE RISK-TAKING MONGOOSE

Therehad been water here before, but in the dry weeks of August the pools had evaporated, leaving on the black cotton soil a thick crust that cracked under the scorching sun. The heat had also turned the remaining grass into lifeless, parched straw. It was evident why the wildebeest were leaving.

Zachariah, Sean, and Ashley rode along, all lost in their own thoughts. The promise of a cold sundowner and a shower at camp after a long day in the sun and dust were strong motivators to get back quickly.

Every animal Zachariah had introduced exhibited a skill that was critical to its survival. Though these skills clearly applied to the competitive world of business, Sean also realized that he needed to teach his children to develop these same skills. The wildebeest and lion had an especially profound impact on him; they made him realize that something as simple as a plan and the tenacity to see it through to the end could help his children achieve most of their goals in life.

Suddenly, a small herd of impalas darted across the road right in front of the Jeep. Zachariah swerved to avoid them, but had to quickly jam on the brakes to prevent hitting them. The dry, sandy surface caused the Jeep to skid a few feet into a termite mound before coming to a halt. Sean and Ashley both jolted forward as a huge dust cloud engulfed them.

"What happened?" Sean asked.

"We ran into an old termite mound, and it's caved in around us."

Zachariah tried to reverse, but the wheels were just spinning up more dust.

"How far are we from camp?" Ashley inquired.

"Not far, maybe three or four miles," Zachariah said, pointing due east over the Musabi plains.

Sean climbed out of the backseat, "Can we walk back?"

"Yes, we can, but I would rather have you two stay here. I can make much better time alone."

"You're going to leave us alone here in the middle of the bush—again?" Ashley responded, with a hint of anxiety.

"I'll be back with Aly and the Rover in a jiffy. You'll be safe in the Jeep. Besides, you're not alone."

"What does that mean?"

Zachariah pointed to another termite mound a short distance away. A whole mongoose family stood up straight on their hind legs atop the mound, surveying the events that had just unfolded before them. The rest, who had rushed to the safety of their burrows, were now also scurrying out to investigate what happened.

"Oh, look, honey, *Meerkat Manor*!" Ashley exclaimed.

Zachariah smiled. He, too, had watched the popular Animal Planet network program that had brought these creatures such fame.

"Almost right, Ashley. The meerkat is predominantly found in southern Africa, but they're from the same family as the mongoose that we have here. Together, they form the largest family of carnivores in the world."

"Carnivores—like lions?"

"Not exactly, but they are meat eaters. However, these guys mostly feed on beetles, grasshoppers, spiders, scorpions, and small rodents. Most folks can relate to the mongoose because they're such social and gregarious animals. They live in groups that usually range in size from 20 to 30 members. They keep in almost constant contact with each other by chattering and twittering among themselves as they go about their daily chores."

Twittering? Interesting choice of words, Sean thought. He smiled at the image of a mongoose tweeting.

Ashley's concern dissipated as she started taking pictures. "One could spend days just watching these little guys. I'll bet you would learn a whole lot about families in the process."

> *"Taking calculated risks is an essential part of every journey."*

"Very much so. They're fun animals to watch. Mongoose packs are led by a dominant alpha pair, and usually produce three litters a year that contain between four and six young. They tend to be very territorial and live in a permanent home that they fiercely protect. In fact, two packs will often fight over territory when they meet, with the larger pack usually chasing the smaller one away.

"Standing upright is their favorite posture. As a precaution, they always have at least one member of the pack standing guard, continuously scanning the ground and the air for danger. At the first hint of danger, the guard will utter a short harsh warning—and the whole group will immediately dash for cover in the mound or the nearest available burrow.

"So, don't worry; this group will certainly let you know if there is anything around. I've got to get going to the camp so I can be back before dark—otherwise Aly will really start wondering where we are."

"What happens if they signal danger?" Sean wanted to know.

"Just stay in the Jeep and you'll be safe. I'll be back within the hour," Zachariah said, as he grabbed a water bottle and a compass and headed out. They watched him make good time as he rapidly put distance between himself and them. Then, they were alone.

Sean and Ashley looked around at the immediate terrain. It was dotted with even more termite mounds than they had initially realized, and the east was filled with spectacular rock formations. A flock of helmeted guinea fowl came scurrying by.

"You know, Ash, this has been the most unusual day of my life—spending it in the bush, witnessing life and death right before our eyes. Nature is truly the greatest heritage we have on this planet. It's a whole different world. It really puts everything we know back home in perspective, doesn't it?"

"I know what you mean."

Sean smiled. It had been many years since the two of them were so at peace and relaxed.

It had been a windy day. In the distance, the dust, backlit by the sun, was creating a colorful palette of intense yellows and oranges, gradually turning red and maroon. The setting sun silhouetted a beautifully shaped acacia tree on the horizon into the well-known indelible trademark of the Serengeti plains.

"Absolutely magnificent," Ashley said. "I have never seen a more spectacular sunset."

As the last of the daylight gave way to the night, the warm sun-bleached sand began to cool rapidly. The animals that favored the light had already taken refuge in anticipation of the nocturnal events that would soon unfold. Evening quickly enveloped the landscape as a tapestry of stars began to emerge in the darkening sky. The wind whistled one last time as if to introduce the sinister sound of the night. Darkness fell fast, as did the temperature.

Sean reached back and found the sweaters they had sported earlier. Though they'd been up now for more than 14 hours, Sean didn't feel tired or stressed—as he often did after a day's work at the office.

"Thank you, Ash," Sean whispered.

"For what?"

"For insisting that we take this trip and come to the Serengeti."

"Oh, *that!*" she chuckled.

After a few minutes, the distant drone of the approaching Land Rover could be heard.

"Has it really been an hour already? That time flew by!"

Sean smiled as he watched the approaching Rover.

"Are you guys alright?" Aly's voice reached them first.

"Everything's fine."

"I was worried to death," Aly said. "We have never left any of our guests alone outside the camp, let alone at night. Zach should never have done this. I am very sorry!"

Sean assured him. "It's fine, don't worry, Aly. It was actually magical for us to be alone with the Serengeti."

"Well, jump in the Rover and let's head back to camp. We'll tow the Jeep to camp in the morning."

Even in the dark, the drive back took less than ten minutes. Aly was still apologizing and giving Zachariah a parental-like scolding as he pulled up in front of the large tent. The camp was much noisier than when they had arrived the previous evening.

Dave and Anthony immediately approached the Rover and began questioning them.

"Sean! What the blazes happened, man?" Dave exclaimed. "This morning you guys weren't here and Aly told us that you went with Zachariah and then he arrives back here on foot tonight without you!"

"We're fine."

"Well, where have you been all day? And what have you been doing?" Dave demanded, as he grabbed Sean and Ashley by the arm and ushered them to the campfire.

"We'd like to shower first," Ashley said.

"Only after we get all the details," everyone insisted at once. Dave brought two glasses of Pinotage as Ashley and Sean settled in near the warmth of the fire.

They recounted the lion hunt, the river crossing, the cheetah kill, the giraffes, the mongoose, and, of course, the crash.

"My goodness," Mary said. "What an incredible day! I hope you realize how lucky you are. We haven't seen a cheetah or a lion kill yet, and we've been here almost a week."

"It was Zachariah. He knew exactly where to go. It was as if the animals were talking to him," Sean replied.

"Ah, our man of intrigue," Dave said.

Sean got up and stood at the edge of the campfire and stared into the flickering flames as he spoke to the group.

"Zachariah is a remarkable thinker with a profound knowledge of the bush and its inhabitants. Remember last night when he told us that we should look at the Serengeti migration in terms of a road map to success, and then went on to explain how the wildebeest uses endurance to overcome their struggle? Well, that was only the first animal skill. There are many, many more."

"How many more?"

"I'm not sure, but today he shared another four—the lion, the crocodile, the cheetah, and the giraffe. It's absolutely amazing how they each demonstrate a unique skill—each vitally important to overcoming their own struggles. Each skill also applies so evidently to our lives—both personally and in business."

"Fill us in," said Anthony.

But before Sean could begin, Zachariah and Aly joined the group, and Dave couldn't resist a little teasing.

"So, Zachariah, on the first day the Californians arrive you leave them terrified and alone in the African bush?"

Before Zachariah could answer, Ashley shot back, "We weren't terrified, just cautious. And it was our second day. *And* we had company and protection."

"What protection?"

"A mongoose family."

"Mongoose? You must be kidding me. Those little animals will run away from anything."

Zachariah's deep, calming voice suddenly filled the air, "Sean and Ashley were completely safe. They were inside the Jeep, close to camp, and in an area not visited by predators. The nearest lions to our camp had just caught a large wildebeest earlier this morning and still had their fill. Furthermore, the mongoose is considerably braver than you think. They are caretakers of one of the seven survival skills of the Serengeti."

"There are seven?" Sean asked, surprised, as he quickly counted them on his fingers, "You've only shared five with us."

Everyone's ears perked up.

"Please tell us about the mongoose's unique survival skill, Zachariah," Ashley asked.

"Well, the mongoose spends the majority of its day searching for food. They are very adventurous and daring—even fearless at times—and will often boldly venture into unknown territory. I've seen a pack join forces to mob an attacker with ferocity you wouldn't expect from little fellows like that."

Raymond added more wood to the fire to take care of the cool evening air. The elusive dancing yellow flame flared up again.

"As a general rule, the mongooses will outmaneuver their predators. They are very quick and agile, and can climb trees and swim if they have to. But it's their courage and willingness to take risks that makes them so unique."

"So risk taking is their unique survival skill," Sean exclaimed.

Zachariah smiled at Sean as he continued. "Life out here doesn't stand still; taking risks is an integral part of everyday survival. If you look closely, taking chances is as normal as breathing. Though our little mongoose is more of a risk taker then most animals his size, make no mistake; he evaluates his options very carefully first."

"I can see how this skill applies to my life. We take risks in business all the time," Sean proclaimed.

"Yes, you do. Even though starting your own company was a huge risk, you did it. Addressing a risk can occasionally paralyze people to the point that they do nothing. Fear of change and the unknown limits us to discover new, exciting, and possibly even superior alternatives.

"To deal with adversity like the mongoose, you need to evaluate all the options before you make your decision.

Are you taking on an acceptable risk? If not, review what you want to achieve and then determine an alternate route that will get you there. The level of risk has a lot to do with the direction you take. Sometimes the path with the highest risk leads to the highest reward."

"But life in America is significantly different than it is out here," Anthony claimed.

"Of course it's different; but *wisdom* isn't. The wisdom lies in the application of the skills."

Zachariah paused to allow the significance of his statement to sit with everyone for a moment. "Consider this question: What do you currently consider impossible?"

"Getting another job," Anthony chuckled.

"Excellent. But it's only impossible because you've limited your options," Zachariah responded.

"What do you mean, limited my options? I've contacted countless employment agencies that serve Wall Street; I've even called some of my former business associates," Anthony protested.

"And those are both great steps—but they're obvious ones. I'm not saying you *shouldn't* do things like that.

But think about it: Have you exhausted all the options both inside and outside your comfort zone?"

"For example?"

"Hmm . . . let's see. Well, how about exploring whether your talents might be put to use overseas? Or, perhaps you could identify a new career with more opportunities than your current one, and retrain yourself with a new skill set? Or explore the purchase of a small business?"

"Wow. Some great options I hadn't considered. I'm not sure they're all feasible however."

"And that's where the calculating part comes in. Taking a risk doesn't mean accepting every option that presents itself. The mongoose would lose his life if he was that reckless. It just means that you have to explore the unknown, remain open to opportunities, and not let fear hold you back," Zachariah responded.

"People who don't shy away from risk take us places we've not yet been. They see how it could be—not how it is. They're willing to reach beyond everyday reality and into the unknown. That means not allowing ourselves to be limited by the social and emotional boundaries, opinions, beliefs, and self-imposed restrictions society establishes."

"I can also see how this applies to our family," Ashley said. "Even though our two daughters are now in their early twenties, if there's one thing parents know for sure—it's the risk that accompanies raising kids. Not a day goes by where you aren't required to weigh options and make decisions that impact your children. Good parents think about the consequences of the decisions they make that affect their children every day."

It all comes down to how you manage life and each decision you make, Sean thought. This risk/reward tune has been played in every classroom, by every professor. When he started the company there was risk, and that continued now, on a daily basis. Zachariah was right. He made choices every day that involved risk.

"We must not fear *fear*, and we need not fear risk. It's well worth it to step outside your comfort zone and make changes. It allows us to realize that life not only consists of changes, but also patterns—roads we've traveled before that are simply called by another name.

"Although I hate to be the one to bring this discussion to an end, I must go and review the data I collected today and prepare for my flight to Masai Mara in the morning. So if you will all excuse me, I'll bid you good night."

"I'm for that. This has been an exciting day but I feel like every pore of my body is filled with dust," Ashley said. "I've been looking forward to my two buckets of shower for a while now."

Everyone chuckled. The Serengeti had also redefined the art of showering.

SKILL 6: RISK TAKING

Summary

Succeeding in troubled times often involves being a *risk taker*. But like the mongoose, you need to evaluate all the options involved with the chance you're taking before you make a decision.

Risk takers frequently review goals and determine the various routes to get to the destination. Often they choose the path with the highest risk in order to gain the maximum reward. Many of them demonstrate the following characteristics:

- The ability to overcome the fear associated with the risk by evaluating potential pitfalls.
- Viewing the change that immobilizes others as simply another hurdle to overcome. Risk takers don't

see how things are, but how they could be. They are willing to do whatever is necessary to achieve the desired goal.

- A readiness to break free from social and emotional boundaries, opinions, beliefs, and restrictions imposed by business and society. Unaffected by the opinions of others, they freely and openly express their ideas.
- Adeptness at finding ways to hedge against risk to take advantage of the upside of a given situation.
- A readiness to assess whether the reward is worth the cost required to take on the risk. They willingly invest hours of personal time on a project, while recognizing that it won't necessarily be successful.
- An upbeat attitude that allows for potential losses and the refusal to be overwhelmed by the prospects.
- The courage to step out into uncharted waters to ensure that goals are achieved.

Everyone has a different comfort level in terms of risk—but no matter how much is involved, a positive attitude is essential for success. If doubts and fears overrule hope and optimism, success is much less likely to occur. Small achievements bolster confidence, which leads to a willingness to take bigger risks and accomplish greater goals.

Maximizing This Skill

The first step in becoming a skillful risk taker is to avoid the two greatest traps that lead to failure: Do not "ignore" the risk, or assume that you can't do anything about it. It's equally important not to intellectualize the risk to the point where you avoid taking action. This will only result in a failure to take ownership and the need to constantly rely upon others. Risk's reward is never available to those who don't even bother to step up to the plate.

Once you have opted to take a gamble, the next step is to diminish any sense of fear by supporting your decision with facts. You must accept the fact that failure is a possible worst-case outcome and then move ahead with enthusiasm and a positive attitude.

Keeping these two thoughts in mind allows the process of taking a risk to become a system of calculating the cost and the benefit before taking any action. Remember: Inside every risk is an opportunity for success.

Chapter 8

THE COMMUNICATING ELEPHANT

There wasn't a cloud in the sky the next morning, and the horizon still included a hint of orange left over from the dawn. The Jeep had already been towed to the camp, and was roadworthy again after receiving some minor repairs.

Aly had offered to take Zachariah to the airstrip, since Raymond had left earlier with Dave, Mary, Anthony, and Cecilia for the sunrise hot air balloon ride. Sean and Ashley had decided to forgo the balloon ride so they could use the opportunity to talk with Zachariah one last time.

The four of them were barely out of the camp when Sean reignited their previous discussion.

"Last night you said there were seven skills, Zachariah. I was counting them over in my bed and could only recall six: the enduring wildebeest, the strategic lion, the enterprising crocodile, the efficient cheetah, the graceful giraffe, and the risk-taking mongoose. What did I fail to remember?"

Zachariah smiled. "You didn't forget anything, Sean. We never saw the animal with the seventh skill."

"Well, then, we must do so before your flight!" Sean declared. "You can't leave us without teaching us *all* the survival skills." Zachariah glanced across to Aly and smiled.

"Well, you folks are very lucky," Aly said, smiling. "Returning with the Jeep this morning, we came across the final caretaker you haven't seen yet. We should be catching up with the herd any minute now."

"Herd of what?" Ashley asked.

"Listen carefully."

Sean and Ashley looked at each other questioningly. They listened, but didn't hear a sound except for the breeze rustling the leaves in the few trees nearby.

It wasn't even nine yet, but they could all tell that it was going to be a very hot day. Sean and Ashley were leaning against opposite sides of the Jeep, gazing out into the bush.

"Are you folks ready for your final lesson?" Zachariah held up his hand. He pointed to their right as Aly pulled off to the side of the road. All Sean and Ashley could hear were some noisy birds—and then a low rumble. As the sound grew louder, it was accompanied by the loud snapping of breaking wood.

Suddenly, a large elephant stepped out of the bush into plain sight. Ashley and Sean gasped as they locked eyes with the largest animal they had ever seen.

"That's the matriarch. She's about 60 years old, and has been roaming this area long before any of us arrived. No member in the herd moves without her say-so."

Sean couldn't take his eyes off the elephant standing a mere 50 yards away from the Jeep—a Jeep that all of a sudden felt very small.

"What's that rumbling I hear?" Sean asked.

"That's their way of communicating with each other. The low frequency sound can be heard for miles. They use a gentle prodding of trunks for emphasis to accompany their rumblings."

"Wow. Now *that's* a very impressive animal," Sean remarked.

"Yes, they are," Zachariah responded. "No other animal, not even the lion, has been the subject of such great interest in history. The elephant has profoundly stirred man's imagination since the beginning of time."

The matriarch raised her trunk in the air, sniffing. Without warning, she started to flap her ears. She lifted her head up, and trumpeted loudly.

And then she charged.

"Aly, let's get out of here!" Ashley shrieked.

"No. Sit still." Aly said calmly.

Ashley instinctively ducked behind the seat in front of her.

After a few steps forward, with her trunk still raised above her head, the elephant came to an abrupt halt in a cloud of dust. Everyone sat motionless.

With ears still flapping and a deafening trumpeting sound, she totally dominated her surroundings. And then as quickly as it had started, it ended.

"What was that?" Sean asked.

"A mock charge," Zachariah said. "A warning for us not to come any closer. Elephants are very gentle animals by nature, when given their space—but get too close, and you're looking for trouble. I suspect her calves must be nearby."

Right on cue, the rest of the herd emerged from behind the tree line. They maintained a strong sense of hierarchy as they crossed over. The older and larger elephants stood in the road between them as the calves crossed behind them. Only after all were safely across the road did the matriarch signal and then retreat.

"Elephants group together in herds, where one female like this old gal—usually the eldest with the most experience—maintains order. They have a unique social structure with clearly defined roles for each animal: caring, sharing, expertise, and protecting the next generation. Those smaller elephants are probably about four to six years old, and will learn all they need to know during their childhood.

"The trunk is an amazing multifunctional piece of equipment comprised of over 10,000 individual muscles. It's sensitive enough to smell water 12 miles away, powerful enough to break a large branch off a tree, yet delicate enough to pluck a single strand of grass."

"I've seen elephants in the circus," Ashley said, "but they look so much larger here."

"At 8,000 pounds, African elephants are the largest animals on earth. Circuses usually use Indian elephants that are about half the size."

"So they sit atop the food chain," Ashley said.

"Although you might think so, they actually don't. Elephants are not predators or carnivores of any kind. They feed off grass, leaves, bark, and fruit, and will occasionally push over a fully grown tree to get at its roots."

"Does that make them vulnerable?"

"Not at all. Being the largest mammal on land means they have no natural enemies—and they've demonstrated the ability to sustain long-term cooperative and mutually beneficial relationships with many of the other animals. Elephants demonstrate a remarkable capacity to converse effectively with one another in order to pass their extensive knowledge down to the next generation. They can receive and interpret some 70 different sounds from each other and their environment. Their communication skills even include humor, mourning, and an ability to lead others."

"Wow—so it's a true learning experience."

"It is. As one of the most intelligent creatures in the world, their brain-to-body mass ratio is second only to humans. They undeniably use their expertise and ability to communicate efficiently."

> *"Effective communication is the art of successfully delivering your message."*

"So, Zachariah, is communication the seventh skill?" Sean asked.

"Yes, it is. As I mentioned, elephants possess a unique ability to communicate with each other through a variety of sounds. It is believed that they can also detect messages through sensitive pads in their feet from as far as 10 miles away. But what makes them even more unique is their ability to communicate through touch. This skill ensures the survival of not only the individual herd, but also the entire species. Communicating the key elements of survival down through the generations by sight, sound, and feel is quite a remarkable ability."

Sean understood well how complex communication really was. Though most people talk, few actually listen—and even fewer have the ability to express themselves effectively so that others can understand them, completely and correctly. Now he was discovering that elephants had mastered the skill of communication. But why was he so surprised? He'd already seen six other animals successfully demonstrate unique skills that could help people succeed in both business and life.

Sean returned to the present with even more interest in his voice than before. "That's amazing. Even though effective communication is clearly a critical skill for success, so many people think they are great communicators when they really aren't. How do I even begin to explain the different facets of this crucial ability to my team?"

"Well," Zachariah said, "Almost all communication is the same, irrespective of the medium. It always involves two people, the sender and the receiver. In order to be successful, the receiver must understand the message in the way that the sender intended. So before you even begin speaking, you must first determine what it is that you wish to say and why. Make sure your message is clear and concise. If it's too lengthy, disorganized, or contains errors, then chances are, it will be misunderstood. If it doesn't match your message, others are likely to misinterpret it.

"Second, you need to determine the most appropriate and effective medium for your message. The advent of technology—including the Internet and social media—has enhanced the available alternatives exponentially. Every medium has its advantages and disadvantages, and should be carefully selected.

"The last thing to do is to try to gain an understanding of the recipient's culture, background, and level of knowledge. Every piece of information will allow you to tailor your message accordingly. Remember that effective communication is the art of mastering words, tone, *and* body language."

"Excellent explanation, Zachariah. You really have mastered these skills," Sean responded. "It's interesting that you touched on nonverbal communication as well. So many people are so focused on the spoken word that they forget it's only one part of communication. They don't always realize that nonverbal expressions play an equally important role."

"Absolutely. Both verbal and nonverbal interactions are magnified even more in business negotiations," Zachariah replied. "And since a key element in negotiation is to favorably influence a decision, you have to completely understand where the other party is coming from."

"And that's so important in our personal lives as well," Ashley offered.

"No question. For a parent or spouse to truly receive a message, they must stop preparing for what they are going to say next and focus on what the other party is verbally and nonverbally communicating. Words often fail to match the nonverbal signals. There are times when we think we hear someone, but we don't completely *listen* to what they're saying."

"Hear that, honey?" Ashley interjected.

Sean shot a glance at Ashley.

Zachariah chuckled. Married life was the same, no matter where you were in the world.

"The most difficult negotiations frequently take place in our personal lives—especially with those we love the most. Emotions—both positive and negative ones—play such an essential role in communication. When our approach is positive, we have more confidence and are more apt to cooperate. This increases the chances that all parties will reach a mutually agreeable solution. On the other hand, a negative, self-centered approach has just the opposite effect—making us more competitive and less cooperative.

"Mastering any skill requires time, effort, and patience. But the seventh skill is especially important, since we spend almost our entire day communicating, negotiating, and making decisions. It's the skill we use the most, and for many people, it's the one that needs the most work. When in doubt, it's often a good idea to ask the person with whom you're interacting what kind of message they received."

They had already been driving for over an hour, when Aly pulled into the clearing at the airstrip where the Cessna was already parked. Their time with Zachariah was almost over.

Sean looked out across the savannah. A mere two days ago, the sights, smells, and sounds had been unfamiliar to him. Now, the pulse of Africa would stay with him forever.

"So, what animal are you?" Sean asked Zachariah.

"Now that you have experienced all the key survival skills, maybe you are able to tell me what you think my dominant skill is."

"Wow, right back to me. Let me see," Sean said, talking aloud to himself. *Endurance like the wildebeest— maybe, strategic like the lion—possibly, the enterprising crocodile—no, gracious giraffe—maybe, efficient like the cheetah—possibly, risk taker like the mongoose—no, and the communicating elephant—possibly. So that narrows it down to the lion, the cheetah, or the elephant. It would take a very strategic mind to uncover and map out these skills, your mentoring abilities are above question, and the efficiency in which you schedule your tasks, track the animals, and monitor their behavior is impressive. So planning, sharing, or organizing.*

143

"Sharing. Mentoring. You are a suburb storyteller. That's it. Great communication is your instinctive survival skill!" Sean exclaimed.

"Excellent observation—and that after only two days in Africa!" Zachariah smiled back. "You're right; I am an elephant."

"Thank you, Zachariah. Ash and I have been blessed to share the past two days with you," Sean said.

"The privilege was all mine. You were willing to learn from nature, and I thank *you* for opening your minds. The migration repeats itself every year; tens of thousands of wildebeest give their lives. But this year, your presence and understanding have provided an additional benefit. The two of you must now go back and share the seven skills with as many people as you can."

"Is any one of the seven skills better than another? What if I feel I have more than one skill? Can I have different skills?" Sean poured with questions.

"Slow down Sean. You still have a way to go on the safari of self-discovery before some of those answers will reveal themselves. Maybe later you can ask Aly to share with you how one finds balance with multiple skills."

"Okay, but before you leave Zachariah you have to tell me what animal am I?" Sean asked.

"Ah, I cannot tell you that; you need to determine that yourself. Though some people never discover who they really are, you have already travelled far. I am confident that you will know soon."

Saying good-bye to Zachariah was surprisingly more difficult than Sean and Ashley had imagined. They exchanged e-mail addresses and promised to stay in touch, but there was an empty feeling inside Sean. The past had suddenly become the present, only to now slip away again.

"Let me know once you figure it out," Zachariah said to Sean. His last words echoed before they closed the plane door and the drowning sound of the propeller made it impossible to hear.

As Ashley walked back to the Jeep, Sean stood on the side of the runway and watched the Cessna take off. He could see Zachariah pressed against the Plexiglas window as he waved one last time.

SKILL 7: COMMUNICATION

Summary

Just as it is for elephants, successful relationships between people—in life and business—depend on good *Communication*. Effective communicators understand that it's not always best to use a lot of words when relaying an idea. In fact, the more words we use, the more our message can be obscured.

Each parcel of words we deliver is accompanied by a nonverbal message that provides insight into the spoken meaning. Skilled communicators understand how critical both verbal and nonverbal exchanges are, and frequently display the following characteristics:

- They're skilled at both listening to and actually *hearing* other people, and taking time to comprehend the details in their message.
- They are interested in advancing the discussion beyond just a series of shared monologues and into a true dialogue. They realize that taking a positive approach can make others feel more confident, and in turn, more likely to cooperate.

Without candid feedback, you have no real way of letting people know how effectively they're accomplishing what they've set out to do—or how they affect you. Some people are willing to accept and even seek feedback, whereas others have a tendency to see it as criticism. Those who prefer to avoid it will often respond negatively. They'll close themselves off, and quickly become inactive listeners.

People who receive feedback openly are truly willing to hear what the other person is saying. They are interested in pursuing the conversation and are genuinely interested in getting others' opinions.

There are two approaches when it comes to giving feedback. An ineffective delivery is aggressive, and focuses on the other person's weaknesses. It is often vague, insensitive, disrespectful, and delivered in a judgmental tone. A positive delivery, on the other hand, focuses on providing valuable and constructive commentary that allows the recipient to effect change. People who provide feedback in a constructive manner are the most capable at truly connecting with—and helping—another person.

Maximizing This Skill

Empathize with the other person's point of view when you're delivering your message, and make a genuine attempt to hear what he or she is saying. Be an active listener by giving and receiving quality feedback. This necessitates thinking before speaking and crafting a reply that addresses the speaker's position and not just your own. It requires that you wait, formulate, and be clear.

Becoming a fruitful communicator requires keeping focus on all four sources of communication:

- Improve verbal communication by concentrating on "hearing" what the other person is attempting to say, and not on your own ideas; listen and respond to their message.
- Ensure that your nonverbal communication—such as gestures, mannerisms, posture, facial expressions, and eye contact—matches your verbal message.
- Good written communication must focus on the axiom that "least is best." Be precise, grammatically correct, clear, and concise—especially when using electronic forms of exchange.
- Effective visual communication involves using photography, signs, symbols, and so forth, that do not confuse your verbal and written message.

Remember, communicating is only effective if both the sender and receiver understand the same information.

Chapter 9

COMING FULL CIRCLE

hat animal *am* I?" Sean thought as he climbed in the back of the Jeep. He smiled at himself; it was the first time he had not instinctively reached for his BlackBerry.

"I was just telling Ashley that we can still make the champagne brunch that we hold after every hot air balloon ride," Aly said.

"Sure, let's do it!" Sean responded, without really listening.

Sensing that Sean was lost in thought, Aly and Ashley continued the drive in silence. They had been driving for less than 10 minutes when they spotted a Land Rover parked in the middle of the open veldt. To the left, only a few yards away, was a table set for six. Right behind it two small tents and tables were set up with gas burners, pots, and pans. A kettle was already boiling on the campfire.

Raymond stepped out of the makeshift cooking tent accompanied by a very enticing aroma.

It was five-star treatment in the middle of the bush. Ashley was amazed at how easily they were able to create comfort and luxury anywhere.

Aly moved to the head of the table and with glass in hand proposed a toast. "Since all of you are leaving tomorrow, it is customary for us to use this opportunity to thank you for coming to visit our world. It is our hope that you will travel safely back to your homes with a piece of the Serengeti forever with you. And that should the opportunity present itself, you will return again one day."

"Hear, hear," everyone echoed.

After everyone had taken a sip, Sean stood up. "First, I believe I speak on everyone's behalf when I convey great thanks to Aly, Raymond, and the rest of the team for their impressive service, impeccable food, and wonderful hospitality. I am not sure what Anthony, Cecilia, Dave, and Mary expected, but I can honestly tell you that Ashley and I have been blown away, and will add this to a short list of the most memorable experiences in our lives. Aly, Raymond, our sincere thanks."

"Hear, hear," everyone echoed again.

"It is always our pleasure to serve our guests and we are very happy that you have enjoyed your time with us."

Sean continued. "Aly, may I ask one more thing?"

"But of course."

"Zachariah said that you would tell me how to find balance with all the multiple survival skills."

"Well, that's a first for my brother."

Sean gasped. "Zachariah is your brother?"

"Yes. He's the oldest of five."

"Well, blow me over," Anthony responded. "Why didn't you tell us the first night that the mystery man is your brother?"

"Time reveals all when it is ready."

Everyone kept silent, staring at Aly.

"The seven skills," he began, "provide exceptional insight into surviving and thriving. Not because we're animals, and not because we should strive to be like them. But in the harsh reality of the Serengeti, life and death dramas have accentuated their unique survival skills in a way that allows us to learn from them. Often, our comfortable existence lets us become complacent—and we fail to identify or grow our skills.

"All who share this planet with us—irrespective of color, race, or religion live to stay alive, reproduce, love, and thrive—much like the animals of the Serengeti. We owe it to all of humanity to live every day to the fullest and to share what we know with those around us.

He continued. "Your unique survival skill is the one you would default to if you were one of the animals living here on the savannahs of the Serengeti. Surviving your own Serengeti requires identifying and using your dominant survival skill to its fullest potential."

In a matter of minutes, Aly had changed. It was as if Aly and Zachariah had become the same person with the same message.

"After you have taken the first step toward discovering your dominant survival skill, you must remember that it is often not just one aptitude that makes the difference between success and failure. Rather, it's an integration of multiple qualities and abilities. Although some rare—and fortunate—individuals have been born with several talents, we frequently have to adapt and learn to expand our skill set. In many cases, companies create teams that are comprised of people with different abilities. Even in marriages and relationships, husbands and wives often complement each other with different skill strengths."

The group sat quiet not saying a word.

"Furthermore, you must constantly strive to improve yourselves throughout the course of your lives. Each of you must be willing to learn from anyone and everyone while accepting the responsibility to share your unique skills to help others—just as each of the animals do. We are all conduits through which life passes; it is our duty both to be mentored and to be a mentor."

"Wow—you've described balance so eloquently," Sean said. "What a huge responsibility."

"And one that I leave you to consider as we head back to camp," Aly concluded.

> *"You must identify your unique survival skill so that you can maximize your full potential."*

That evening, after packing their bags, Sean and Ashley sat in their five-star, three-room tent reminiscing about the exhilarating few days.

Ashley put her arms around Sean. "Ready to go back to your problems in California? After all, I did promise they'd still be there when we got back."

"They definitely feel much less insurmountable now. I am actually looking forward to applying the new insights I gained."

"Is that right?" Ashley teased. "So the trip was worthwhile?"

"Worthwhile? It was remarkable and awe-inspiring," Sean exclaimed. "I never anticipated that this trip would turn into a journey of self-discovery. It was very humbling! I have many skills I need to relearn, master, and share.

"I am also going to miss the wide open savannahs, the incredible sunsets, extraordinary animals, and the warm, welcoming flicker of the campfire," Sean said somewhat sadly.

"I completely understand. I've fallen in love with this place, too, and with the 'old you' it's brought back," she said, giving him another hug. "You seem to have regained your drive and energy."

Sean did, indeed, feel rejuvenated.

"I would never have guessed that Zach and Aly are brothers. Very surprising. Makes sense though. I wish we'd had more time with Zach. I still feel I have so much more I could learn."

"What's great is that you and I now have a new perspective. We can refocus on what's important. There are so many things that we take for granted, didn't do right, or didn't even know existed. We have so much to be grateful for—our health, our children, and our friends. Let's go to bed now. I'm exhausted."

"Soon," Sean said. "I just need to figure out what animal I am."

"I am sure you will."

"What do you think I am?" Sean asked.

After pausing for a few seconds, Ashley responded. "You could be a wildebeest. You have unbelievable tenacity. Or a cheetah. Your organizational skills are amazing, and everyone knows you're super efficient. But then maybe you're an elephant, like Zach. You are a gifted communicator."

"So, which one?"

"The dominant one, you mean?" Ashley asked, yawning. "I'm not sure. Anyway, Zach said you had to figure it out yourself."

"Just reflecting."

"Well, let's go to sleep now and you can wonder more tomorrow."

"And what animal are you, Ash?"

"Tomorrow, honey. Good night."

"Good night, Ash."

Sean lay in bed listening to the growing sounds of the approaching night. Many of them now were old friends: the high-pitched laugh of the hyena, the low growl of a far off lion, and the thundering hooves of wildebeest on the move.

EPILOGUE

The Following Evening

Zachariah was perched high on a rock in the Masai Mara reserve in Kenya, some 200 miles northeast of where the wildebeest had crossed the Grumeti River yesterday. Here in the northern part of the Serengeti it had been raining for the last few weeks and the grasslands were now a stunning paradise.

In a few days the first of the wildebeest herds would be arriving from the south, anxious to feed on the lush, green grass. He delighted in observing the annual migration—it made him feel alive.

He also loved being one with nature. A tapestry of stars began to unfold against a rich gold and crimson horizon. Tonight was another picture perfect evening.

Unexpectedly, he felt his iPhone vibrate. It was a message from Sean; he and Ashley were at the airport in Narobi en route to the United States and his BlackBerry had reception again.

There was only one word on the screen.

C-h-e-e-t-a-h.

Zachariah smiled with satisfaction.

Sean had completed the next step in his journey of self-discovery.

WHAT ANIMAL AM I?

If you are willing to listen, nature has much to share.

The many solitary hours I spent on the Serengeti plains of East Africa gave me the chance to observe how nature maintains its unique balance. It can seem ruthless at times, and we're often unable to comprehend it. I will be the first to acknowledge that I do not understand it all, either. Yet I have come to appreciate the value of the lessons we can learn by looking more closely than we normally do. It is through my experiences that I am able to explain these seven skills—an explanation that will hopefully contribute to your personal journey.

First, let me share some basic principles:

- There are herbivores, carnivores, and omnivores. Herbivores eat grass and other plants, carnivores eat herbivores and other meat, and omnivores eat almost anything.
- Collectively and individually, animals live according to a very strict code that includes many predetermined realities of life. Each accepts the others for who they are and the role they play in the world around them.
- Each species struggles not only with its own need to survive, but also its natural instinct to reproduce and thrive—the very essence of the circle of life.

While the challenges faced by those that live and die on the Serengeti plains are certainly in a different realm than ours, the seven survival skills that the animals use to overcome their harsh conditions can help us rise above our own adversities and live a better life.

Hopefully, this book has helped you discover what unique survival skill you possess. If you are still not sure, take the following online quick quiz at: www.WhatAnimalAmI.com.

AFRICAN WILDLIFE
FOUNDATION

The African Wildlife Foundation (AWF), together with the people of Africa, work to ensure the wildlife and wild lands of Africa will endure forever.

Founded in 1961, this global conservation organization operates in three unique but overlapping areas: conserving wildlife, protecting land, and empowering people.

Its unique approach to conservation is to protect areas that serve as ecological and economic anchors of much larger landscapes. One such area, the Masai Steppe Heartland, is home to the Serengeti plains of East Africa and the annual wildebeest migration.

It is with deep gratitude for its commitment and dedication to the wildlife and wild lands of Africa, that a percentage of each sale of *Surviving Your Serengeti* will go to the AWF.

THE SERENGETI PLAINS
OF EAST AFRICA

The Great Annual Migration

ACKNOWLEDGMENTS

Tom Mitchell, you are all over this book. I am eternally grateful for your passion and unwavering commitment.

To my two sons, Tinus and DJ, I could not ask for more. Thank you for your support and the pleasure of working with you on this book. May it always remind you of the skills required to succeed and the importance of following your dreams.

One always holds a very special place for those that believed in you when uncertainty prevailed. Your support fueled this journey more than you will ever know: My sincere appreciation to Mark Willis, Ron and Alexander Siegel, Sean Buvala, Dale Stinton, and Cassie Hillinger.

I also carry a deep gratitude for the many thousands of clients and supporters I have met in the real-estate industry over the years, whether at events, in business, or online. Many of you have become friends and made my immigration to the Unites States two decades ago an enjoyable ride. Had it not been for all of you, this stage of my life would not have been possible. Mahalo!

More recently, and more specifically tied to this book, a few individuals—Steve Harrison, Brendon Buchard, Dr. John Ullmen, and Jay Papasan—influenced the development of *Surviving Your Serengeti*. Your guidance contributed to the progress and refinement of the message and your influence served to introduced me to many new relationships that, in turn, provided encouragement and valuable information—such as Elizabeth, Carla, Sandra, Logan, David, Terri, Lorrie, Camper, Wendy, Laura, and Jill—may each of you succeed in business and life!

Behind every successful book there is a dedicated team of literary agents, editors, publicists, and consultants. To my team—Ethan Friedman (Level Five Media), Richard Narramore (John Wiley & Sons, Inc.), Barbara Henricks, Rusty Shelton, Kevin Small, Tim and Titus Keiningham, Luke Williams, and to anyone else that I have not mentioned by name—thank you!

And the biggest appreciation goes to Era, my wife of 30 years. Thank you for allowing me the many, many hours to follow my dream—I love you!

ABOUT THE AUTHOR

Stefan Swanepoel was born in the Serengeti (Kenya, Africa) and spent the first 35 years of his life in Kenya, Hong Kong, and South Africa. As the son of a diplomat, he is well versed in travel and has had firsthand experience in over 30 countries around the world.

His academic accomplishments include a bachelor's degree in science, a master's in business economics, and diplomas in arbitration, mergers and acquisitions, real estate, computer science, and marketing. He has served as CEO of seven companies and two nonprofits.

Stefan has written 19 books on business trends, real estate, and social media, and is widely acknowledged as the leading expert on real estate business trends, and has been listed as "One of the Top 100 Most Influential People in Real Estate."

Today he is a keynote speaker, captivating audiences worldwide. He has presented over 700 talks to over 400,000 people.

Stefan lives with his wife and two sons in California.

More information on Stefan:

www. Swanepoel.com

Twitter: www.Twitter.com/Swanepoel
Facebook: www.Facebook.com/Swanepoel
LinkedIn: www.LinkedIn.com/Swanepoel

More information on this book:

www.SerengetiBook.com

Twitter: www.Twitter.com/Serengeti
Facebook: www.Facebook.com/Serengeti
YouTube: www.YouTube.com/SerengetiBook